The Standa
0 Introduction

This is The Standard. A collection of decades of experience in the engineering industry. I authored it to help you find your way through the wide ocean of knowledge. The Standard is not perfect and never will be, and it reflects the ongoing evolution of the engineering industry. While it may be written by one person, it is the collection of thoughts from hundreds of engineers that I've had the honor to interact with and learn from throughout my life.

The Standard holds hundreds of years of collective experiences from many different engineers. As I have traveled the world and worked in various industries, I've had the chance to work with many kinds of engineers - some of them were mad scientists who would fixate on the smallest details of every single routine. And some others have been business engineers who cared more about the end results than the means to get to these results. In addition to others, I've learned from all of them: what makes a simple engineering guide that can light the way for all other engineers to be inspired by it and hopefully follow it. And therefore, I have made this Standard, hoping it will be a compass for engineers to find the best way to engineer solutions that will hopefully change the world.

This Standard is an appeal to engineers worldwide: read through it and make extracts of their experiences and knowledge to enrich an engineering Standard worthy of the industry of software. We live today knowing the origins of the earth, of man, and all the animals. We know how hot boiling water is; how long, a yard. Our ships' masters know the precise measurements of latitude and longitude. Yet, we have neither chart nor compass to guide us through the wide sea of code. The time has come to accord this great craft of ours with the same dignity and respect as the other standards defined by science.

The value of this Standard IS immense for those in the industry who are still finding their way or even those who have lost their way, and the Standard can guide them towards a better future. But more importantly, The Standard is written for everyone, equally, to inspire every engineer or engineer-to-be to look forward to focusing on what matters the most about engineering--its purpose, not its technicalities. When engineers have any form of Standard, I have observed that they start focusing more on what can be accomplished in our world today. And when a team of engineers follows some form of Standard, their energy and focus become more about what can be accomplished, not how it should be accomplished.

I collected, then authored this Standard, hoping it will eliminate much of the confusion and enable engineers to focus on what matters most--use technology as a means for higher purposes and to establish its equivalent goals. The art and science of designing software have come a long way and have proven to be one of the most powerful tools a person could have today. It deserves a proper introduction, and how we educate youth about it matters.

In essence, The Standard is my interpretation of SOLID principles and many other practices and patterns that continue to enrich our designs and development to achieve truly solid systems. The Standard aims to help every engineer find guidance in their day-to-day work. But more importantly, the Standard can ensure every engineer that when they need to build rugged systems that can land on the moon, solve the most complex problems, and ensure the survival of humankind and its evolution--they have the guidance required.

The Standard is intentionally technology-agnostic. Its principles can apply to any programming language, and its tri-nature of foundation can guide any development or design decisions beyond software. I will be using C# on the .NET framework to only materialize and realize the concepts of this Standard. But know that at the early stages of forming this Standard, I was heavily using Scala as a programming language. The Standard shall not be tied to any particular technology, nor shall it be a limitation to those who want to follow it, regardless of their language of preference. But what's more important about The Standard? It's also meant to play the role of inspiration for generations of engineers to come to either follow it, improve on it, or come up with their own. The alternative is to build software without standards, which is subject to chaos and injustice when it comes to investing the best time into the best efforts. Our industry today is in chaos in terms of standardization. Unqualified individuals may have or take leadership positions and influence those who are much more qualified to make unfortunate decisions. The Standard is the option to set a measure for expertise, influence, and knowledge depth before making any decisions.

The Standard is also my labor of love for the rest of the world. It is driven by and written with a passion for enhancing the engineering experience and producing efficient, rugged, configurable, pluggable, and reliable systems that can withstand any challenges or changes as it occurs almost daily in our industry.

[*] Introduction to The Standard

[*] Questions about The Standard

0.0 The Theory
0.0.0 Introduction

When designing any system, it is of utmost importance for the designer to backup their design with a certain theory. Theories play a massive role in ensuring the purposes, models and simulations of their design are cohesive and extensible within a certain domain.

Any system out there regardless of how chaotic it may seem is mandatorily influenced by at least one theory either coined by the designer or inherited from previous designers or their systems.

Regardless of what or who the influencer may be, it is important for the designer to fully understand the theory they follow or it will negatively impact their future decisions in terms of extending their design to keep up with a forever changing and expanding universe.

I have realized early on that the simpler any theory is, the easier it becomes for other designers to adapt the theory and extend it's reach beyond the original designer's dreams. A universe built on top of simpler patterns can make it a lot easier for those who marvel at its beauty to better understand it and appreciate it much more than those who just give-in to the fact that it's complex beyond their comprehension.

A theory about the universe could make life much more purposeful, enriched with all sorts of tales about survival, evolution and fulfillment.

0.0.1 Finding Answers

Early on in my life, I struggled with schooling. Nothing that was taught made any sense to me. It seemed that everyone at school was more concerned with memorizing and regurgitating what they've memorized during their exam than truly understanding consciously what was being taught and question it's origins and validate it's purposes.

I realized at an earlier age that I needed some magical equation to help me distinguish between what's true and what's not. What's right and wrong. What's driven by a purpose and what's an imitation for those who have true purposes.

So, I started my search in coming up with a theory that can explain the world to me. I was named all kinds of names during my schooling years. But I didn't mind much of that because my heart, mind and body were fully invested into finding the answer to everything.

When looking for answers, it's important to keep your heart and mind open for all the options. Don't let any social or traditional structures limit your mind from seeking the truth about the universe and embracing the answers from everywhere.

After years and years of search, I settled on a theory that made it simple for a simple person like myself to understand everything. I called it The Tri-Nature of Everything.

0.0.2 Tri-Nature

The Tri-Nature theory states that everything in this world is comprised of 3 main categories. Dependencies, purposes and exposures. Each one of these components plays a crucial role towards the survival of its system, its evolution and fulfillment.

Let's talk about these components here.

0.0.2.0 Purpose

Everything around us has a purpose. It was created and designed with a certain reason in the mind of it's creator. We design cars to take us from point A to point B. We design cups for drinking, plates for eating and shoes for walking. Everything in existence has a core purpose the governs it's design and legitimizes it's existence.

0.0.2.1 Dependency

But every system out there must have a dependency in one form or another in order. For instance, we as biological systems rely on food and water to survive. Cars rely on oil or electricity. Computer systems rely on power and electricity and so on. Every system no matter how small or big it may be, and regardless of it's impact and importance must have a dependency of some kind.

0.0.2.2 Exposure

But in order for a dependency to become a dependency it needs to expose itself somehow for other systems to rely on it. For instance, power outlets are an exposure layer for power sources to allow other systems to plug in and consume its services. Gas stations are exposure layers for oil tanks buried underground to store that oil. And so on with every system out there it needs to expose itself to allow other systems to integrate with it and consume its capabilities.

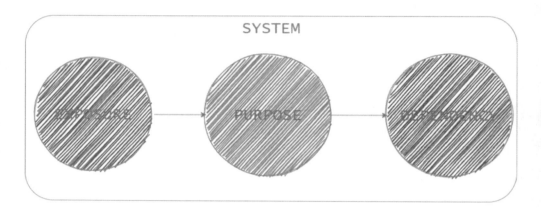

0.0.3 Everything is Connected

In the larger scheme of things, all systems out there are connected to one another. A simple example of this is the food chain in nature. The sun is a dependency for the grass to grow, grasshoppers are consumers of grass while frogs feed on grasshoppers then snakes would feed off of frogs and so on.

Every single member in the food chain is a system that has dependencies, purposes and exposure.

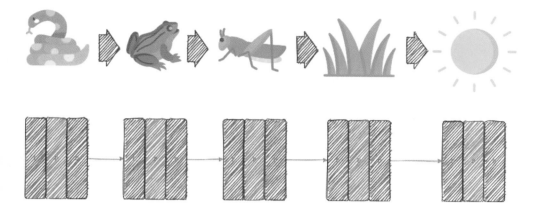

Since computer systems are nothing but a reflection of our reality. These systems integrations represent a chain of infinite dependencies each one of these systems relies on one or more systems to fulfill its purpose. A simple mobile application could rely on a backend system to persist it's data. But the backend system relies on cloud-based system to store the data. And the cloud based system relies on file system to perform basic persistance operations and so on.

0.0.4 Fractal Pattern

The Tri-Nature pattern could also be perceived at the lowest scale of any system as well as the highest scale. That's what we call a fractal pattern. Every system out there is infinity comprised of three components each one of them has three components as well and so on.

For instance, the smallest known component in the universe are the quarks within neutron within an atom. these quarks are three components, two down quarks and one up quark. but if you zoom out slightly you would see the larger system where these quarks reside is also comprised of three components which are the electrons, protons and neutrons.

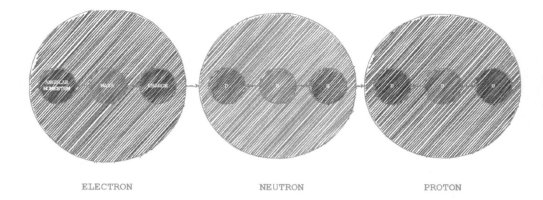

ELECTRON   NEUTRON   PROTON

If we zoom far out from the sub-atomic level to the solar system, the pattern continues to repeat itself at a massive scale. Our solar system is comprised of a sun, planets and moons. and they fall exactly within the dependency purposing and exposure patterns as the components in the sub-atomic level as follows:

And if we zoom further out at scale, we find out that galaxies are made out of dust, gas and dark matter.

The Tri-Nature pattern continues to repeat itself into every aspect of our lives. Every component in our universe from the smallest sub-atomic parts to a massive scale galaxies and solar systems the follow the same rule.

0.0.5 Systems Design & Architecture

It is now evident that a good theory that we can follow to design systems has been discovered! We can now develop every single component in our software with accordance to The Tri-Nature of Everything. The rules and guidelines that govern designing software according to The Theory is called The Standard. It refers to the universal standard in designing systems in every matter.

The Standard dictates at the low-level architecture that every system out there should be comprised of brokers (dependencies) and services (purposes) and exposers (exposures).

For instance, when designing a simple RESTful API, we may need to integrate with a database system, then validate incoming data based on certain business rules then expose these capabilities to the outside world for the API consumers to be able to integrate with it.

According to The Standard that system would look like this:

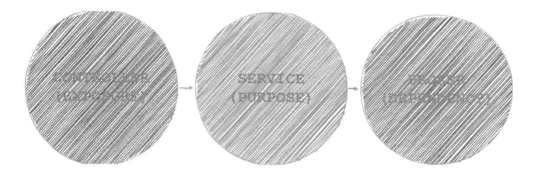

When digging deeper into any of these components, the same pattern would repeat itself. For instance, a service is comprised of validation components, processing components and integration components. And then if we zoom in a bit further, these very validation components are comprised of three finer components which are the structural validations, the logical validations and external validations. The pattern continues to go on and on to the lowest level of our design as shown here:

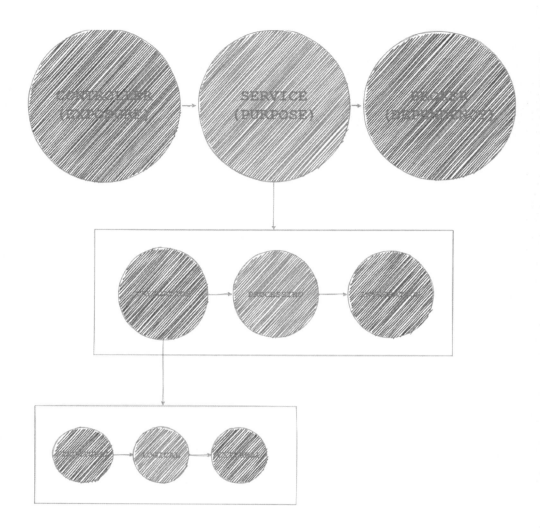

The same pattern also applies to larger systems if we zoom out of the one system realm into distributed modern systems such as microservice architectures - the same pattern should apply as follows:

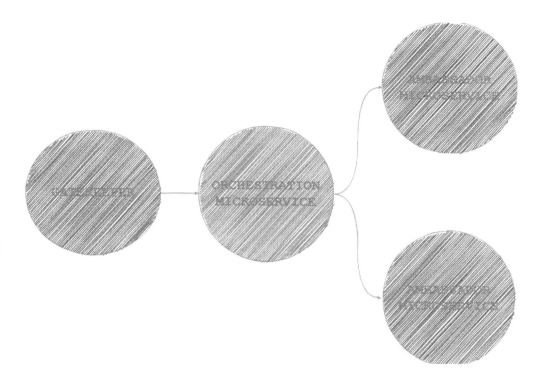

In a distributed system, some services play the role of ambassadors to external or local resources which is the equivalent of a broker component at the service level. But then a purpose-driven component must come into play to orchestrate business flows by combining one or many primitive resource-consumption operations from these ambassador services. The final part which is the exposure layer, a thin gatekeeper layer that becomes the first point of contact between the outside world and your microservice architecture.

The same pattern of tri-nature will continue to repeat itself across several systems may it be large across multiple organizations or small within one single service.

0.0.6 Conclusion

In conclusion, The Tri-Nature of Everything is the theory that powers up The Standard. Every single aspect in the rules and guidelines of The Standard are heavily influenced by The Tri-Nature theory. But it's important to understand that the theory goes well beyond designing some software system. It can apply to management styles, writing books, making meals, establishing relationships and every other aspect of our lives which goes beyond the purpose of The Standard here.

It is quite evident now after so many years of research and experimentation with the Tri-Nature theory that it works! It helps simplify some of the most complex systems out there. It plays well with our intuition as human beings, and makes it even simpler for automatons in the future to expedite our development processes of software and hardware and everything else in between.

Finally, The Standard is an ongoing journey of continuing to question The Tri-Nature theory. The further we go into uncharted waters in terms of business domains the more we discover some new territories where my theory still stands. Even for the most chaotic systems out there the theory applies in certain ways even if the components of said systems didn't quite adhere to The Standard form of distinction.

0.1 Purposing, Modeling and Simulation
0.1.0 Introduction

The Standard defines the process of software engineering in three main categories. Purposing, Modeling and Simulation. Each one of these aspects plays a crucial role in guiding the efforts of engineering towards producing a successful solution and fulfilling a particular purpose.

The order in which these aspects are followed is also intentional. A purpose must exist to shape the modeling process. And one can't simulate interactions with no models. But while that order at the initiation of the engineering process is crucial, It's important to understand that the process itself is selectively iterative. A change in the purpose may reflect as a change in the simulation but not necessarily the modeling. A change in the models may not neccessarily require a change in either the purpose nor the simulation.

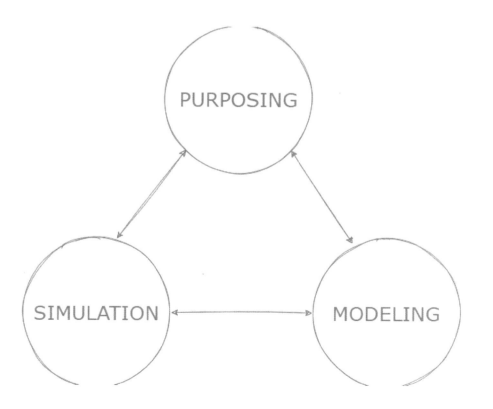

0.1.1 Purposing

The purposing process is our ability to find out *why* we need a solution. For instance, if we are having an issue with knowing how many items are on the shelf in some grocery store. We deem the manual process of counting to be inefficient and a system needs to be put in place to ensure we have the proper count of items.

Purposing therefore, is to find a reason to take an action. Reasoning relies heavily on observability. Our ability to observe problems and then being able to articulate the problem to better device a solution that addresses the given problem.

So, we have the observation, the articulation of the reasoning (the problem) and the intent for a solution. All of these aspects constitute the Purposing portion of engineering software.

0.1.1.0 Observation

We live in a world full of observables. Our inspiration is triggered by our ambition to achieve more. Our dreams reveal blockers in our way that we need to solve to continue our journey and fulfill our dreams. From the moment a young student uses a calculator to solve a complex equation to the moment that very student becomes an astronaut, calculatoring the trajectory of satellites orbiting our planet.

Observation is our ability to detect an issue that's blocking a goal from being achieved. Issues can be as simple as coming up with the proper count of items on a grocery store shelf. All the way up to understanding why we can't capture images of planets millions of light years away from us. These are all what engineers would describe an observable problem.

The greater the purpose, the more complex a problem is going to be. But these smaller purposes are our way to train our minds to tackle bigger ones. Step by step, one problem at a time.

0.1.1.1 Articulation

Describing the observable is an art in and of itself. Because describing a problem properly is half way to its solution. The clearer the articulation of the problem is, the more likely the problem is to be understood by others helping us to solve that very same problems.

Articulation isn't always with words. It's also with figures and shapes. It is not an accident that some of the most advanced ancient cultures have used figures and shapes to describe their times and their history. Figures are a universal language, understood and interpreted by anyone who could relate to them much faster than learning a spoken language. In fact, a figure or shape might be the most optimum way to illustrate an idea as it pictures are worthy of thousands of words.

Articulation requires the passion to solve the issue. Whether it's written, said or illustrated. A passionate mind shall convey the hidden message of the criticality of the problem to be solved. Articulating a problem is a big part of how one can sell their solution. Our ability to convey an idea towards other engineers and then those who will be investing and using this solution is one of the most important aspects of engineering software.

0.1.1.2 Solutioning

A part of the purpose is the way to fulfil it. In the engineering industry, fulfilling the goals can't just be by -any- means. A huge aspect of why so many massive pieces of software fails around the world is because the solutioning aspect was overlooked as a trivial part of the purpose. You may have heard of those who were pressured against a deadline so they decided to cut corners to achieve the goal. In our Standard, this is a violation. A solution *mu st* be not just fulfilling to a goal, but it must be a purpose in and of itself. This is in terms of optimization, readability, configurability and longevity. Solutioning as part of the purpose is software craftmanship.

0.1.2 Modeling

Modeling is the second most important aspect of software engineering. It's our ability to extract models from the actors in any problem. Whether these actors are living beings, objects or other. For instance, in a problem where we are trying to count the items on a grocery store shelf, a model would be for these items. Extracting only the attributes that are relevant to the problem we are trying to solve, and discarding everything else.

A simpler example would be detecting the items in a grocery store that are perishable. The only attribute we are concerned with here is the expiration date on the item. Everything else including the label, color, weight or any other details are out of the scope of the modeling process and the solution.

Modeling then cannot exist without a purpose. As the purpose defines the scope or the framework of which the modeling should occur. Modeling without a purpose leaves the door open for attracting infinite number of attributes every single element in the observable universe may have.

The relationship between the purposing and modeling attributes is proportional. The more complex the purpose is, the more likely the modeling process will require more attributes from the real world to resemble in a prototype.

We express our models in programming languages as a `class`. The aforementioned perishable items problem above can be represented as follows:

```
public class Item
{
    public DateTimeOffset ExpirationDate {get; set;}
}
```

The name of the `class` represents the overall *type* of the item. Since all items have the exact same attribute of `ExpirationDate` then the name shall stay as generic as it can be.

Now, imagine if our purpose grew a bit more complex. Let's assume the new problem is to be able to identify the more expensive perishable items so the store can put them up front for selling before the less expensive items. In this case our model would require a new attribute such as `Price` so a computer program or a solution can determine which is more valuable. This is how our new model would look like:

```
public class Item
{
    public double Price {get; set;}
    public DateTimeOffset ExpirationDate {get; set;}
}
```

0.1.2.0 Model Types

Models govern the entire process of simulating a problem (and its solution). Models themselves break into three main categories, Data Carriers, Operational and Configurations. Let's discuss those types in the following sections:

0.1.2.0.0 Data Carrier Models

Data carrier models have one main purpose which is to carry data points across systems. Data carrier models can vary based on the type of data they carry. Some data carrier models will carry other models to represent a complex system. Some others will just represent references to the original data points it represents.

Data carrier models in a relational fashion can be broken into three different categories. These categories makes it a lot clearer what the areas of priority are in terms of development, design and engineering. For instance, we can't start developing secondary/supporting models if we don't have our primary models in place first. Let's talk about these categoris in details:

0.1.2.0.0.0 Primary Models

Primary models are the pillars of every system. Any given system cannot proceed in terms of design and engineering without a clear definition and a materialization of these primary models. For instance, if we are building a schooling system, models like `Student`, `Teacher` and `Course` are considered Primary models.

We call these models Primary because they are self-sufficient. They don't rely physically on some other model in order for them to exist. Which means that a given Primary model like `Student` may still exist in a schooling system whether a `Teacher` record existed or not. This is called physical dependency. Primary models in a relational storage schema do not contain any foreign keys or references to any other physical model.

Primary models however may rely conceptually or logically on other models. For instance, a `Student` model has a logical relationship to a `Teacher`. Simply because there can never be a student without a teacher and vice versa. A `Student` model also has a conceptual relationship with its host and neighboring hosting services. For instance, there's a conceptual relationship between a `Student` model and a `Notification` model in terms of business flow. Any given student in any school conceptually relies on notifications to attend certain classes, complete certain assignments or any other events.

0.1.2.0.0.1 Secondary Models

Secondary models on the other hand, have a hard-dependency on Primary models. In a relational database model, secondary models usually have foreign keys referencing another model in the overall database schema. But even in non-relational storage systems, secondary models can be represented as nested entities within a given larger entity or have a loose reference to another entity.

Let's talk about some examples for secondary models. a `Comment` model in a social media platform cannot exist without a `Post` model. You simply cannot comment on something that doesn't exist. In a relational database, the comments model would look something like this:

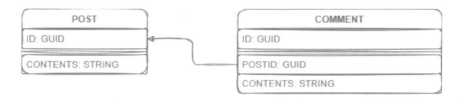

In the example above, a secondary model `Comment` has a foreign key `PostId` referencing the primary key `Id` in a `Post` model. In a non-relational system, secondary models can easily be identified as nested objects within a given entity. Here's an example:

```
{
  "id": "some-id",
  "content": "some post",
  "comments": [
    {
      "id": "comment-id",
      "content": "some comment"
    }
  ]
}
```

Secondary models in general may have logical and conceptual relations to other models within their host, neighboring or external systems. However, their chances of having these conceptual relations are much less than the Primary models.

0.1.2.0.0.2 Relational Models

Relational models are connectors between two Primary models. Their main responsibility is to materialize a many-to-many relationship between two entities. For instance, a `Student` may have multiple teachers; and a `Teacher` may have multiple students. In this case an intermediary model.

Relational models are not supposed to have any details in them. They only contain references to other models and that is their primary key. A composite key that aggregates two or more foreign keys within it. Let's take a look at an example:

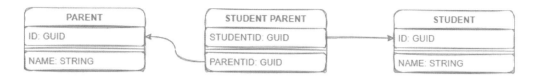

0.1.2.0.0.3 Hybrid Models

There's a situation where a model is connecting multiple entities but is also carrying its own data. I highly advise against following that path to maintain a level of purity in your system design and control the complexity of your models. However, sometimes this approach is a necessary option to proceed with a certain implementation or a business flow. In which case, we can propose a hybrid model that can carry certain details about the relationship between two independent entities.

Here's an example of a hybrid model that can occur in reality. In a soft-delete scenario, a hybrid model can describe the detachment between two entities in a many-to-many relationship. Let's assume a group member does not want to be a part of a certain group anymore. We consider their group membership as `Deactivated` with a reason attached without actually fully delete the record. Here's how would that look like:

In a non-relational data model the referencing integrity might become a bit more looser given the linear nature of that schema. Hybrid models combine both secondary models in the way they reference Primary models, and they implement a relational nature in which they allow multiple entities to relate to each other with no exclusivity.

0.1.2.0.1 Operational Models

Operational models mainly target the simulation aspect of any software system. Think about all primitive, complex and exposure operations a simple scenario could require for a successful simulation to be implemented. Let's assume we are trying to solve a problem where we can simplify students registrations in some school. The registration process will require some simulation to add these students information into a computerized system.

Operational models will handle the exposure, processing and integration of that entire process, by offering services that offers APIs/UIs to enter, post, add and insert/persist students information into some schooling system.

Operational models can be broken into three main categories, which are: Integration, Processing and Exposure. The Standard focuses heavily on operational models because they represent the core of any system in terms of business flows. Operational models are also where most of the resources of development and design go in any software development effort.

Let's talk the operational models here.

0.1.2.0.1.0 Integration Models (Brokers)

Integration operational models main responsibility is to connect any existing system with external resources. These resources can be localized to the environment of that system like reading the current date or time or remote like calling an external API or persisting data in some database.

We call these integration models Brokers. They play the role of a liaison between processing operational models and external systems. Here's an example:

```
public partial class ApiBroker
{
    public async ValueTask<Student> PostStudentAsync(Student student) =>
        this.apiBroker.PostAsync<Student>(student, url);
}
```

The integration model above, offers a capability to call an external API, while abstracting the configuration details away from the processing operational models.

Just like any other operational model type, they don't hold data within them, but rather use private class members and constants to share internal data across it's public and private methods. The `ApiBroker` here as a model represents a simulation of integration with an external system.

We will discuss Brokers extensively in upcoming chapters to shed some light on the rules and guidelines in developing brokers with any external resources or systems.

0.1.2.0.1.1 Processing Models (Services)

Processing models are the holders of all business-specific simulations. Things like student registrations, requesting a new library card or simply retrieving some student information based on a certain criteria. Processing models themselves can be either primitive/foundational, high-order/processing or advanced/orchestrators.

Processing models in general either rely on integration models, or self-relying like computational processing services or rely on each other.

Here's an example of a simple foundational/primitive service:

```
public partial class StudentService : IStudentService
{
  private readonly IStorageBroker storageBroker;
  ...

  public async ValueTask<Student> AddStudentAsync(Student student) =>
    await this.storageBroker.InsertStudentAsync(student);
}
```

A higher-order service would do/look as follows:

```
public partial class StudentProcessingService : IStudentProcessingService
{
  private readonly IStudentService studentService;
  ...

  public async ValueTask<Student> UpsertStudentAsync(Student student)
  {
    ....

    Student maybeStudent = await this.studentService
      .RetrieveStudentByIdAsync(student.Id);

    return maybeStudent switch
    {
      null => await this.studentService.AddStudentAsync(student),
      _ => await this.studentService.ModifyStudentAsync(student)
    }
  }
}
```

A more advanced orchestration-type services would combine from multiple processing or foundational services as follows:

```
public partial class StudentOrchestrationService : IStudentOrchestrationService
{
  private readonly IStudentProcessingService studentProcessingService;
  private readonly IStudentLibraryCardProcessingService studentLibraryCardProcessingService;
  ...

  public async ValueTask<Student> RegisterStudentAsync(Student student)
  {
    ....
    Student upsertedStudent = await this.studentProcessingService
      .UpsertStudentAsync(student);

    ...

    await this.studentLibraryProcessingService.AddStudentLibraryCardAsync(studentLibraryCard);
  }
}
```

In general, operational models are only concerned with the nature of simulation or processing of certain data carrier models, they are not concerned with withholding data, neither retaining a status. In general, operational models are stateless in the sense that they don't retain none of the details that went through them other than delegating logging for observability and monitoring purposes.

0.1.2.0.1.2 Exposure Models (Exposers)

Exposure models handle the HMI in all scenarios where a human and a system have to interact. They could be simple RESTful APIs, they could be SDKs or just UI like in web, mobile or desktop applications including commandline-based systems/terminals.

Exposure operational models are just like the integration models, they allow the outside world to interact with your system. They sit on the other end of any system and they are responsible for routing every request, communication or call to the proper operational models. Exposure models never communicate directly with integration models, and they don't have any configuration within them other then their dependencies being injected through their constructors.

Exposure models may have their own language in terms of operations, for instance, an integration model might use a language like `InsertStudent` while an exposure model for an API endpoint would use a language such as `PostStudent` for express the very same operation in an exposure context.

Here's an example for exposure models:

```
public class StudentsController
{
    private readonly IStudentOrchestrationService studentOrchestrationService;

    [HttpGet]
    public async ValueTask<ActionResult<Student>> PostStudentAsync(Student student)
    {
        Student registeredStudent = await this.studentOrchestrationService
            .RegisterStudentAsync(student);

        return Ok(registeredStudent);
    }
}
```

The above model exposes an API endpoint for RESTful communication to offer a capability to register students into some schooling system. We will be discussing further the types of exposure models based on the context and the system they are implemented within.

0.1.2.0.2 Configuration Models

The last type of models in any system are the configuration models. They can represent the entry point in any system, or register dependencies for any system or simply play the role of middleware to route URLs into their respective function within an exposure model.

Configuration models usually sit at the beginning of launching a system, or handling incoming and ongoing communications or simply handle underlying system operations like memory caching, thread management and so on.

In a simple API application you may see models that look like this:

```
public class Startup
{
    public void ConfigureServices(IServices services)
    {
        services.AddTransient<IStorageBroker, StorageBroker>();
        services.AddOAuth();
    }
}
```

As you can see the code snippet above, the configuration model `Startup` offers capabilities to handle dependency injection-based registration of contracts to their concrete implementations. They may handle adding security or setting up a middleware pipeline. Configuration models are technology-specific. They may differ from a Play framework in Scala to a Spring or Flex in Python or Java. We will outline high-level rules according to The Standard for configuration models but we will not dive deeper into the details of implementing any of it.

0.1.3 Simulation

The simulation aspect of software engineering, is our ability to resemble the interactions to and from the models. For instance, in the grocery store example, a simulation would be the act of *selling* the item. Selling the item requires multiple modifications to the item in terms of deducting the count of the available items and reordering the items left based on the most valuable available item.

The simulation process can be described as illustrating the relationships between models. they are programmed as `functions`, `methods` or `routines` and these all mean the same thing. If we have a software service that is responsible for items sales, a simulation process would look like this:

```
public class SaleService
{
    public void Sell(Item item) => Items.Remove(item);
}
```

In the example above, we have a model called `SaleService` that offers a functionality to simulate the sales process in the real world on a model of an item. And this is how you describe everything in object-oriented programming. Everything is an object (from a model) and these objects interact with each other (simulation).

Objects interacting in general can be observed in three different types. A model taking an action on another model. For instance, the `SaleService` is executing an action of `Sell` on an `Item` model. That's a model interacting with another model. In the very same example, a simulation could be something happening to the model from another model such as the `Item` in the aforementioned example. And the last type of simulation is a model interacting with itself. Models that self-dispose once their purpose is fulfilled and they are no longer needed for example. They will self-destruct.

The simulation process is the third and last aspect of software engineering. Which we will dive deeply in when we talk about brokers, services and exposers to illustrate how the modeling and simulation process happens in the industrial software.

0.1.4 Summary

If we considered purposing to be the domain or the framework in which models interact. Then the following illustration should simplify and convey the picture a bit clearer:

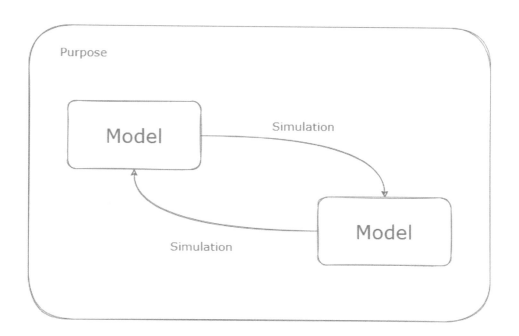

It's important to understand that a computer software can serve multiple purposes. Computer software can interact with other software that share common purposes. The purpose of the software becomes the model and the integrations becomes the simulations in that aspect. Here's a 10,000 feet example:

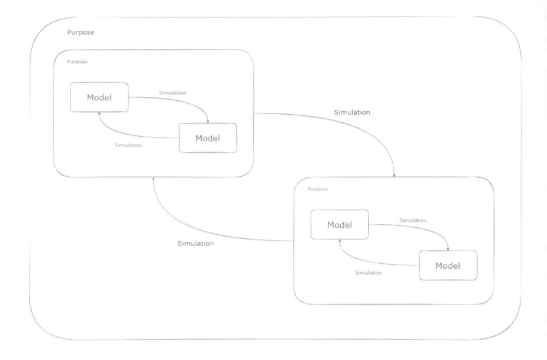

The complexity of any large system can be very easily broken down into smaller problems if the single-purpose or single-responsibility aspect was enforced for each and every sub-system. That's what modern software architectures would call granularity and modularization. Which we will be discussing briefly throughout the architecture aspect of The Standard.

[*] Purposing, Modeling & Simulation (Part 1)

0.2 Principles

In this chapter, we will explore the principles of The Standard. These principles apply to all components in Standard-compliant system. Whether these components are brokers, services or exposers.

0.2.0 People-First

The main idea of this principle is to build and design Standard-compliant systems with people in mind. Not just the people who are going to utilize the system but also the people who are going to be maintaining and evolving it.

In order for a system to follow the people-first principle it must honor simplicity over complexity. Simplicity leads to rewritability. It also leads to designing monolithic systems that are built with modulus mindset to allow a true fractability in the overall pattern of the system.

The Standard also enforces the principles of measuring advanced engineering concepts against the understanding of mainstream engineers. New engineers in the industry are the leaders of tomorrow. If they are not buying in on any system they'll eventually give-up and rewrite it over and over again.

0.2.0.0 Simplicity

Code written according to The Standard has to be simple. There are measures to ensure this simplicity takes place, these measures are as follows:

0.2.0.0.0 Excessive Inheritance

Any software written according to The Standard shall not have more than one level of inheritance. Over one level of inheritance will be considered excessive and prohibited. Except in cases of versioning for the vertical scaling of flows. Excessive inheritance has proven itself over the years to be a source of confusion and difficulty in terms of readability and maintainability.

0.2.0.0.1 Entanglement
0.2.0.0.1.0 Horizontal Entanglement

Building "common" components in every system with the promise to simplify
the development process is another prohibited practice in Standard-
compliant systems. This practices manifests itself in components with names
like Utils, Commons or Helpers. These terminologies and what they imply
in terms of false promised simplifications are not allowed. Any system built
according to The Standard should be comprised of Brokers, Services or
Exposers, nothing more or less.

Another example of horizontal entanglements are shared models across
multiple independent flows - sharing exceptions, validation rules or any other
form of entanglement across multiple flows.

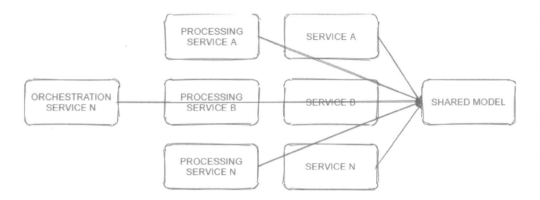

0.2.0.0.1.1 Vertical Entanglement

This principle also applies to scenarios where base components are used.
Unless these base components are native or external they will not be allowed
in a Standard-compliant system. Local base components create a vertical
level of entanglement that harms the maintainability and readability of code.
Vertical entanglements are just as harmful as Commons components that
create single points of failure across any system.

Entanglements (vertical or horizontal) also prevent engineers in any system
(especially newcomers) from fully understanding the depth of the system and
fully own it's functionality. They also prevent engineers from having the
opportunity to build end-to-end flows when half of the functionality is
presumably componentized for the sake of development expedition and
simplicity.

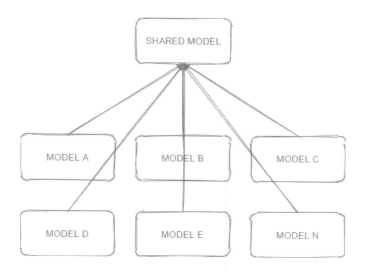

0.2.0.0.2 Autonomous Components

This principle favors duplication over presumed simplification via code entanglement. Every component in every system should be self-sufficient. Every component implements it's own validations, tooling and utilities in one of it's dimensions with no hard-dependency on any other external components except through dependency injection.

Autonomous components will open up the opportunity for every single engineer on every team to fully own every dependency and tool their component may need to fulfil it's purpose. This may cause a bit of duplication in some of the code for the sake of opening an equal opportunity for every developer to fully learn how to build and evolve a component.

0.2.0.0.2.0 No Magic

Autonomous components put all their routines up in front of the engineer. No hidden routines, shared libraries or magical extensions that require chasing references once an inevitable split of the big monolith begins to occur.

We will treat Objects the way they are in nature. multi-dimensional components that are self-containerized like atoms in nature. These components perform their own validations, exception handling, tracing, security, localization and everything else in between.

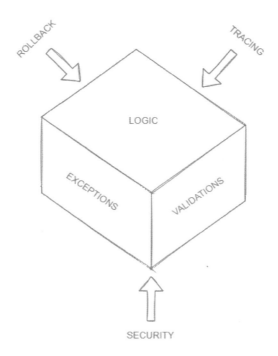

Components built according to The Standard strictly adheres to the idea of *W hat You See Is What You Get* (WYSIWYG) - everything concerning the components will be on the component itself.

0.2.1 Rewritability

Every system should be developed with the rewritability principle in mind. The principle dictates that our assumptions in the systems we develop has the high potentiality of being reexamined and probably reconsidered. Every system out there should be easily rewritable as a measure of adherence to a forever growing and changing business requirements.

Rewritable code is code that is easy to understand, modify and fully rewrite. Rewritable code is extremely modular and autonomous it encourages engineers to evolve it with the least amount of effort and risk possible.

Rewritable code doesn't play tricks on the reader. There are no hidden dependencies, injected routines at runtime nor unknown prerequisites. It should be plug-n-play - fork, clone, build and run all it's tests successfully with no issues.

0.2.2 Mono-Micro

Building monolithic systems with modular mindset. Every flow should be built fully independent from other flows. For instance, we may build a monolithic system with microservice mindset. Which means that any flow can be extracted out of the system and turned into it's own microservice or lambda with the least amount of effort possible.

This principle goes hand in hand with the concept of autonomous components at a higher-level where flows are also autonomous from their neighboring flow and their hosting system.

0.2.3 Level 0

Code must be understandable by an entry-level individual in the engineering craft. Our code base continues to live only based on how easy it is to understand by the mass majority of engineers in the industry. The mass-majority of engineers in our industry will always be those who are new in the craft.

Level 0 engineers are our measure of success. Their ability to understand our code is our reassurance that this very code will continue to live and evolve with the next generation of engineers.

This principle also mandates every engineer in the industry to cross-examine their code and pair with juniors in the field to see if they meet this principle.

0.2.4 Open Code

Open code as a principle dictates that everything written according to The Standard should be commonly available to the public. Developing internal tools that is not accessible shall inevitably harm the engineering experience for those who are trying to evolve these very tools. This applies to internal artifactory practices, on-trial libraries and any other form of module development that doesn't allow every engineer everywhere to learn and evolve any given system.

This principle also recognizes that there are cases where code cannot be open or publicly available for certain purposes. And acknowledges that tooling, platforms and patterns that are not meant to be common should not be made available to the public in certain circumstances.

0.2.5 Airplane Mode (Cloud-Foreign)

The Standard enforces the idea of airplane mode. Where engineers can stand-up their entire infrastructure on their local machine without needing or having any form of network connection. This principle goes heavily against principles such as Cloud-Native applications where a given system cannot stand and run without cloud infrastructure.

The Standard also encourages it's adapters to develop the proper tooling to bridge the gap between cloud infrastructural components and local components such as queues, event hubs and any other tools to make it easily testable and modifiable.

0.2.6 No Toasters

The Standard shall be taught man to man not machine to man. There should be no stylecops or analyzers implemented to force people into following The Standard. It should be driven by passion in the heart and conviction in the mind. The Standard should be taught by people to people. It's meant to foster an engineering culture of open discussions, conviction and understanding.

1 Brokers
1.0 Introduction

Brokers play the role of a liaison between the business logic and the outside world. They are wrappers around any external libraries, resources, services or APIs to satisfy a local interface for the business to interact with these resources without having to be tightly coupled with any particular resources or external library implementation.

Brokers in general are meant to be disposable and replaceable - they are built with the understanding that technology evolves and changes all the time and therefore they shall be at some point in time in the lifecycle of a given application be replaced with a modern technology that gets the job done faster.

But Brokers also ensure that your business is pluggable by abstracting away any specific external resource dependencies from what your software is actually trying to accomplish.

For instance, let's say you have an API that was built to consume and serve data from a SQL server. At some point in time, you decided that a better more economical option for your API is to rely on a NoSql technology instead. Having a broker to abstract away the dependency on SQL will make it so much easier to simply integrate with NoSql with the least time and cost humanly possible.

1.1 On The Map

In any given application, mobile, desktop, web or simply just an API - brokers usually reside at the "tail" of any app - that's because they are the last point of contact between our custom code and the outside world.

Whether the outside world in this instance is just simply a local storage in memory, or an entirely independent system that resides behind an API, they all have to reside behind the Brokers in any application.

In the following low-level architecture for a given API - Brokers reside between our business logic and the external resource:

1.2 Characteristics

There are few simple rules that govern the implementation of any broker - these rules are:

1.2.0 Implements a Local Interface

Brokers have to satisfy a local contract. they have to implement a local interface to allow the decoupling between their implementation and the services that consume them.

For instance, given that we have a local contract `IStorageBroker` that requires an implementation for any given CRUD operation for a local model `Student` - the contract operation would be as follows:

```
public partial interface IStorageBroker
{
    IQueryable<Student> SelectAllStudents();
}
```

An implementation for a storage broker would be as follows:

```
public partial class StorageBroker
{
    public DbSet<Student> Students { get; set; }

    public IQueryable<Student> SelectAllStudents()
    {
        using var broker = new StorageBroker(this.configuration);

        return broker.Students;
    }
}
```

A local contract implementation can be replaced at any point in time from utilizing the Entity Framework as shows in the previous example, to using a completely different technology like Dapper, or an entirely different infrastructure like an Oracle or PostgreSQL database.

1.2.1 No Flow Control

Brokers should not have any form of flow-control such as if-statements, while-loops or switch cases - that's simply because flow-control code is considered to be business logic, and it fits better the services layer where business logic should reside not the brokers.

For instance, a broker method that retrieves a list of students from a database would look something like this:

```csharp
public IQueryable<Student> SelectAllStudents()
{
    using var broker = new StorageBroker(this.configuration);

    return broker.Students;
}
```

A simple function that calls the native EntityFramework DbSet<T> and return a local model like Student.

1.2.2 No Exception Handling

Exception handling is somewhat a form of flow-control. Brokers are not supposed to handle any exceptions, but rather let the exception propagate to the broker-neighboring services where these exceptions are going to be properly mapped and localized.

1.2.3 Own Their Configurations

Brokers are also required to handle their own configurations - they may have a dependency injection from a configuration object, to retrieve and setup the configurations for whichever external resource they are integrating with.

For instance, connection strings in database communications are required to be retrieved and passed in to the database client to establish a successful connection, as follows:

```csharp
public partial class StorageBroker : EFxceptionsContext, IStorageBroker
{
    private readonly IConfiguration configuration;

    public StorageBroker(IConfiguration configuration)
    {
        this.configuration = configuration;
        this.Database.Migrate();
    }

    protected override void OnConfiguring(DbContextOptionsBuilder optionsBuilder)
    {
        string connectionString = this.configuration.GetConnectionString("DefaultConnection");
        optionsBuilder.UseSqlServer(connectionString);
    }
}
```

1.2.4 Natives from Primitives

Brokers may construct an external model object based on primitive types passed from the broker-neighboring services.

For instance, in e-mail notifications broker, input parameters for a `.Send(...)` function for instance require the basic input parameters such as the subject, content or the address for instance, here's an example:

```
public async ValueTask SendMailAsync(List<string> recipients, string subject, string content)
{
    Message message = BuildMessage(recipients, ccRecipients, subject, content);
    await SendEmailMessageAsync(message);
}
```

The primitive input parameters will ensure there are no strong dependencies between the broker-neighboring services and the external models. Even in situations where the broker is simply a point of integration between your application and an external RESTful API, it's very highly recommended that you build your own native models to reflect the same JSON object sent or returned from the API instead of relying on nuget libraries, dlls or shared projects to achieve the same goal.

1.2.5 Naming Conventions

The contracts for the brokers shall remain as generic as possible to indicate the overall functionality of a broker, for instance we say `IStorageBroker` instead of `ISqlStorageBroker` to indicate a particular technology or infrastructure.

But in case of concrete implementations of brokers, it all depends on how many brokers you have providing similar functionality, in case of having a single storage broker, it might be more convenient to maintain the same name as the contract - in our case here a concrete implementation of `IStorageBroker` would be `StorageBroker`.

However, if your application supports multiple queues, storages or e-mail service providers you might need to start be specifying the overall target of the component, for instance, an `IQueueBroker` would have multiple implementations such as `NotificationQueueBroker` and `OrdersQueueBroker`.

But if the concrete implementations target the same model and business value, then a diversion to the technology might be more befitting in this case, for instance in the case of an `IStorageBroker` two different concrete implementations would be `SqlStorageBroker` and `MongoStorageBroker` this case is very possible in situations where environment costs are reduced in lower than production infrastructure for instance.

1.2.6 Language

Brokers speak the language of the technologies they support. For instance, in a storage broker, we say `SelectById` to match the SQL `Select` statement and in a queue broker we say `Enqueue` to match the language.

If a broker is supporting an API endpoint, then it shall follow the RESTFul operations language, such as `POST`, `GET` or `PUT`, here's an example:

```
public async ValueTask<Student> PostStudentAsync(Student student) =>
    await this.PostAsync(RelativeUrl, student);
```

1.2.7 Up & Sideways

Brokers cannot call other brokers. that's simply because brokers are the first point of abstraction, they require no additional abstractions and no additional dependencies other than a configuration access model.

Brokers can't also have services as dependencies as the flow in any given system shall come from the services to the brokers and not the other way around.

Even in situations where a microservice has to subscribe to a queue for instance, brokers will pass forward a listener method to process incoming events, but not call the services that provide the processing logic.

The general rule here then would be, that brokers can only be called by services, and they can only call external native dependencies.

1.3 Organization

Brokers that support multiple entities such as Storage brokers should leverage partial classes to break down the responsibilities per entities.

For instance, if we have a storage broker that provides all CRUD operations for both `Student` and `Teacher` models, then the organization of the files should be as follows:

- IStorageBroker.cs
    - IStorageBroker.Students.cs
    - IStorageBroker.Teachers.cs
- StorageBroker.cs
    - StorageBroker.Students.cs
    - StorageBroker.Teachers.cs

The main purpose of this particular organization leveraging partial classes is to separate the concern for each entity to even a finer level, which should make the maintainability of the software much higher.

But brokers files and folders naming convention strictly focuses on the plurality of the entities they support and the singularity for the overall resource being supported.

For instance, we say `IStorageBroker.Students.cs`. and we also say `IEmailBroker` or `IQueueBroker.Notifications.cs` - singular for the resource and plural entities.

The same concept applies to the folders or namespaces containing these brokers.

For instance, we say:

```
namespace OtripleS.Web.Api.Brokers.Storages
{
    ...
}
```

And we say:

```
namespace OtripleS.Web.Api.Brokers.Queues
{
    ...
}
```

1.4 Broker Types

In most of the applications built today, there are some common Brokers that are usually needed to get an enterprise application up and running - some of these Brokers are like Storage, Time, APIs, Logging and Queues.

Some of these brokers interact with existing resources on the system such as time to allow broker-neighboring services to treat time as a dependency and control how a particular service would behave based on the value of time at any point in the past, present or the future.

1.4.0 Entity Brokers

Entity brokers are the brokers providing integration points with external resources that the system needs to fulfill a business requirements.

For instance, entity brokers are brokers that integrate with storage, providing capabilities to store or retrieve records from a database.

Entity brokers are also like queue brokers, providing a point of integration to push messages to a queue for other services to consume and process to fulfill their business logic.

Entity brokers can only be called by broker-neighboring services, simply because they require a level of validation that needs to be performed on the data they receive or provide before proceeding any further.

1.4.1 Support Brokers

Support brokers are general purpose brokers, they provide a functionality to support services but they have no characteristic that makes them different from one system or another.

A good example of support brokers is the `DateTimeBroker` - a broker made specifically to abstract away the business layer strong dependency on the system date time.

Time brokers don't really target any specific entity, and they are almost the same across many systems out there.

Another example of support brokers is the `LoggingBroker` - they provide data to logging and monitoring systems to enable the system's engineers to visualize the overall flow of data across the system, and be notified in case any issues occur.

Unlike Entity Brokers - support brokers may be called across the entire business layer, they may be called on foundation, processing, orchestration, coordination, management or aggregation services. that's because logging brokers are required as a supporting component in the system to provide all the capabilities needed for services to log their errors or calculate a date or any other supporting functionality.

You can find real-world examples of brokers in the OtripleS project here.

1.5 Implementation

Here's a real-life implementation of a full storage broker for all CRUD operations for `Student` entity:

For IStorageBroker.cs:

```
namespace OtripleS.Web.Api.Brokers.Storage
{
    public partial interface IStorageBroker
    {
    }
}
```

For StorageBroker.cs:

```
using System;
using EFxceptions.Identity;
using Microsoft.EntityFrameworkCore;
using Microsoft.Extensions.Configuration;
using OtripleS.Web.Api.Models.Users;

namespace OtripleS.Web.Api.Brokers.Storage
{
    public partial class StorageBroker : EFxceptionsContext, IStorageBroker
    {
        private readonly IConfiguration configuration;

        public StorageBroker(IConfiguration configuration)
        {
            this.configuration = configuration;
            this.Database.Migrate();
        }

        protected override void OnConfiguring(DbContextOptionsBuilder optionsBuilder)
        {
            string connectionString = this.configuration.GetConnectionString("DefaultConnection");
            optionsBuilder.UseSqlServer(connectionString);
        }
    }
}
```

For IStorageBroker.Students.cs:

```
using System;
using System.Linq;
using System.Threading.Tasks;
using OtripleS.Web.Api.Models.Students;

namespace OtripleS.Web.Api.Brokers.Storage
{
    public partial interface IStorageBroker
    {
        public ValueTask<Student> InsertStudentAsync(Student student);
        public IQueryable<Student> SelectAllStudents();
        public ValueTask<Student> SelectStudentByIdAsync(Guid studentId);
        public ValueTask<Student> UpdateStudentAsync(Student student);
        public ValueTask<Student> DeleteStudentAsync(Student student);
    }
}
```

For StorageBroker.Students.cs:

```csharp
using System;
using System.Linq;
using System.Threading.Tasks;
using Microsoft.EntityFrameworkCore;
using Microsoft.EntityFrameworkCore.ChangeTracking;
using OtripleS.Web.Api.Models.Students;

namespace OtripleS.Web.Api.Brokers.Storage
{
    public partial class StorageBroker
    {
        public DbSet<Student> Students { get; set; }

        public async ValueTask<Student> InsertStudentAsync(Student student)
        {
            using var broker = new StorageBroker(this.configuration);

            EntityEntry<Student> studentEntityEntry =
                await broker.Students.AddAsync(entity: student);

            await broker.SaveChangesAsync();

            return studentEntityEntry.Entity;
        }

        public IQueryable<Student> SelectAllStudents()
        {
            using var broker = new StorageBroker(this.configuration);

            return broker.Students;
        }

        public async ValueTask<Student> SelectStudentByIdAsync(Guid studentId)
        {
            using var broker = new StorageBroker(this.configuration);

            broker.ChangeTracker.QueryTrackingBehavior =
                QueryTrackingBehavior.NoTracking;

            return await broker.Students.FindAsync(studentId);
        }

        public async ValueTask<Student> UpdateStudentAsync(Student student)
        {
            using var broker = new StorageBroker(this.configuration);

            EntityEntry<Student> studentEntityEntry =
                broker.Students.Update(entity: student);

            await broker.SaveChangesAsync();

            return studentEntityEntry.Entity;
        }

        public async ValueTask<Student> DeleteStudentAsync(Student student)
        {
            using var broker = new StorageBroker(this.configuration);

            EntityEntry<Student> studentEntityEntry =
                broker.Students.Remove(entity: student);

            await broker.SaveChangesAsync();

            return studentEntityEntry.Entity;
        }
    }
}
```

1.6 Summary

Brokers are the first layer of abstraction between your business logic and the outside world, but they are not the only layer of abstraction. simply because there will still be few native models that leak through your brokers to your broker-neighboring services which is natural to avoid doing any mappings outside of the realm of logic, in our case here the foundation services.

For instance, in a storage broker, regardless what ORM you are using, some native exceptions from your ORM (EntityFramework for instance) will occur, such as `DbUpdateException` or `SqlException` - in that case we need another layer of abstraction to play the role of a mapper between these exceptions and our core logic to convert them into local exception models.

This responsibility lies in the hands of the broker-neighboring services, I also call them foundation services, these services are the last point of abstraction before your core logic, in which everything becomes nothing but local models and contracts.

1.7 FAQs

During the course of time, there have been some common questions that arose by the engineers that I had the opportunity to work with throughout my career - since some of these questions reoccurred on several occasions, I thought it might be useful to aggregate all of them in here for everyone to learn about some other perspectives around brokers.

1.7.0 Is the brokers pattern the same as the repository pattern?

Not exactly, at least from an operational standpoint, brokers seems to be more generic than repositories.

Repositories usually target storage-like operations, mainly towards databases. but brokers can be an integration point with any external dependency such as e-mail services, queues, other APIs and such.

A more similar pattern for brokers is the Unit of Work pattern, it mainly focuses on the overall operation without having to tie the definition or the name with any particular operation.

All of these patterns in general try to achieve the same SOLID principles goal, which is the separation of concern, dependency injection and single responsibility.

But because SOLID are principles and not exact guidelines, it's expected to see all different kinds of implementations and patterns to achieve that principle.

1.7.1 Why can't the brokers implement a contract for methods that return an interface instead of a concrete model?

That would be an ideal situation, but that would also require brokers to do a conversion or mapping between the native models returned from the external resource SDKs or APIs and the internal model that adheres to the local contract.

Doing that on the broker level will require pushing business logic into that realm, which is outside of the purpose of that component completely.

Brokers do not get unit tested because they have no business logic in them, they may be a part of an acceptance or an integration test, but certainly not a part of unit level tests - simply because they don't contain any business logic in them. We define business logic code as any intended sequential, selective or iteration code.

1.7.2 If brokers were truly a layer of abstraction from the business logic, how come we allow external exceptions to leak through them onto the services layer?

Brokers are only the *the first* layer of abstraction, but not the only one - the broker neighboring services are responsible for converting the native exceptions occurring from a broker into a more local exception model that can be handled and processed internally within the business logic realm.

Full pure local code starts to occur on the processing, orchestration, coordination and aggregation layers where all the exceptions, all the returned models and all operations are localized to the system.

1.7.3 Why do we use partial classes for brokers who handle multiple entities?

Since brokers are required to own their own configurations, it made more sense to partialize when possible to avoid reconfiguring every storage broker for each entity.

This is a feature in C# specifically as a language, but it should be possible to implement through inheritance in other programming languages.

1.7.4 Are brokers the same as providers (Provider Pattern)?

No. Providers blur the line between services (business logic) and brokers (integration layer) - brokers are targeting particular components within the system that are disposable. Providers seem to include more than just that.

2 Services
2.0 Introduction

Services in general are the containers of all the business logic in any given software - they are the core component of any system and the main component that makes one system different from another.

Our main goal with services is that to keep them completely agnostic from specific technologies or external dependencies.

Any business layer is more compliant with The Standard if it can be plugged into any other dependencies and exposure technologies with the least amount of integration efforts possible.

2.0.0 Services Operations

When we say business logic, we mainly refer to three main categories of operations, which are validation, processing and integration.

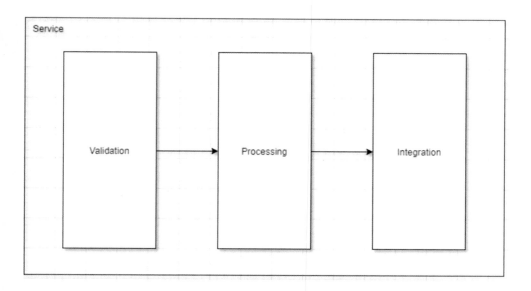

Let's talk about these categories.

2.0.0.0 Validations

Validations focus on ensuring that the incoming or outgoing data match a particular set of rules, which can be structural, logical or external validations, in that exact order of priority. We will go in details about this in the upcoming sections.

2.0.0.1 Processing

Processing mainly focuses on the flow-control, mapping and computation to satisfy a business need - the processing operations specifically is what distinguishes one service from another, and in general one software from another.

2.0.0.2 Integration

Finally, the integration process is mainly focused on retrieving or pushing data from or to any integrated system dependencies.

Every one of these aspects will be discussed in details in the upcoming chapter, but the main thing that should be understood about services is that they should be built with the intent to be pluggable and configurable so they are easily integrated with any technology from a dependency standpoint and also be easily plugged into any exposure functionality from an API perspective.

2.0.1 Services Types

But services have several types based on where they stand in any given architecture, they fall under three main categories, which are: validators, orchestrators and aggregators.

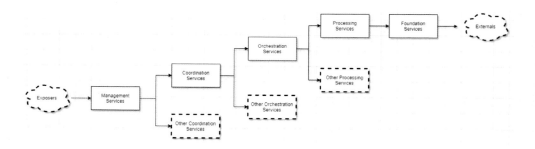

2.0.1.0 Validators

Validator services are mainly the broker-neighboring services or foundation services.

These services' main responsibility is to add a validation layer on top of the existing primitive operations such as the CRUD operations to ensure incoming and outgoing data is validated structurally, logically and externally before sending the data in or out of the system.

2.0.1.1 Orchestrators

Orchestrator services are the core of the business logic layer, they can be processors, orchestrators, coordinators or management services depending on the type of their dependencies.

Orchestrator services mainly focuses on combining multiple primitive operations, or multiple high-order business logic operations to achieve an even higher goal.

Orchestrators services are the decision makers within any architecture, they are the owners of the flow-control in any system and they are the main component that makes one application or software different from the other.

Orchestrator services are also meant to be built and live longer than any other type of services in the system.

2.0.1.2 Aggregators

Aggregator services main responsibility is to tie the outcome of multiple processing, orchestration, coordination or management services to expose one single API for any given API controller, or UI component to interact with the rest of the system.

Aggregators are the gatekeepers of the business logic layer, they ensure the data exposure components (like API controllers) are interacting with only one point of contact to interact with the rest of the system.

Aggregators in general don't really care about the order in which they call the operations that is attached to them, but sometimes it becomes a necessity to execute a particular operation, such as creating a student record before assigning a library card to them.

We will discuss each and every type of these services in detail in the next chapters.

2.0.2 Overall Rules

There are several rules that govern the overall architecture and design of services in any system.

These rules ensure the overall readability, maintainability, configurability of the system - in that particular order.

2.0.2.0 Do or Delegate

Every service should either do the work or delegate the work but not both.

For instance, a processing service should delegate the work of persisting data to a foundation service and not try to do that work by itself.

2.0.2.1 Two-Three (Florance Pattern)

For Orchestrator services, their dependencies of services (not brokers) should be limited to 2 or 3 but not 1 and not 4 or more.

The dependency on one service denies the very definition of orchestration. That's because orchestration by definition is the combination between multiple different operations from different sources to achieve a higher order of business-logic.

This pattern violates Florance Pattern

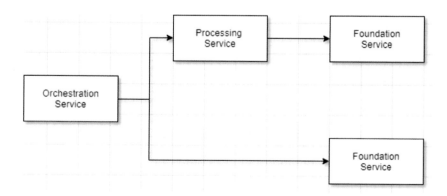

This pattern follows the symmetry of the Pattern

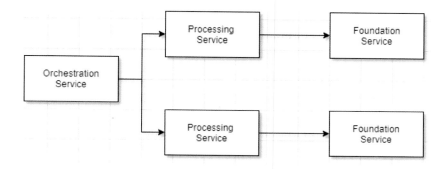

The Florance pattern also ensures the balance and symmetry of the overall architecture as well.

For instance, you can't orchestrate between a foundation and a processing service, it causes a form of unbalance in your architecture, and an uneasy disturbance in trying to combine one unified statement with the language each service speaks based on their level and type.

The only type of services that is allowed to violate this rule are the aggregators, where the combination and the order of services or their calls doesn't have any real impact.

We will be discussing the Florance pattern a bit further in detail in the upcoming sections of The Standard.

2.0.2.2 Single Exposure Point

API controllers, UI components or any other form of data exposure from the system should have one single point of contact with the business-logic layer.

For instance, an API endpoint that offer endpoints for persisting and retrieving student data, should not have multiple integrations with multiple services, but rather one service that offers all of these features.

Sometimes, a single orchestration, coordination or management service does not offer everything related to a particular entity, in which case an aggregator service is necessary to combine all of these features into one service ready to be integrated with by an exposure technology.

2.0.2.3 Same or Primitives I/O Model

For all services, they have to maintain a single contract in terms of their return and input types, except if they were primitives.

For instance, a service that provides any kind of operations for an entity type `Student` - should not return from any of its methods any other entity type.

You may return an aggregation of the same entity whether it's custom or native such as `List<Student>` or `AggregatedStudents` models, or a primitive type like getting students count, or a boolean indicating whether a student exists or not but not any other non-primitive or non-aggregating contract.

For input parameters a similar rule applies - any service may receive an input parameter of the same contract or a virtual aggregation contract or a primitive type but not any other contract, that simply violates the rule.

This rule enforces the focus of any service to maintain it's responsibility on a single entity and all it's related operations.

Once a service returns a different contract, it simply violates it's own naming convention like a `StudentOrchestrationService` returning `List<Teacher>` - and it starts falling into the trap of being called by other services from a completely different data pipelines.

For primitive input parameters, if they belong to a different entity model, that is not necessarily a reference on the main entity, it begs the question to orchestrate between two processing or foundation services to maintain a unified model without break the pure-contracting rule.

If the combination between multiple different contracts in an orchestration service is required, then a new unified virtual model has to be the new unique contract for the orchestration service with mappings implemented underneath on the concrete level of that service to maintain compatibility and integration safety.

2.0.2.4 Every Service for Itself

Every service is responsible for validating its inputs and outputs. You should not rely on services up or downstream to validate your data.

This is a defensive programming mechanism to ensure that in case of swapping implementations behind contracts, the responsibility of any given services wouldn't be affected if down or upstream services decided to pass on their validations for any reason.

Within any monolithic, microservice or serverless architecture-based system, every service is built with the intent that it would split off of the system at some point, and become the last point of contact before integrating with some external resource broker.

For instance, in the following architecture, services are mapping parts of an input Student model into a LibraryCard model, here's a visual of the models:

Student

```
public class Student
{
    public Guid Id {get; set;}
    public string Name {get; set;}
}
```

LibraryCard

```
public class LibraryCard
{
    public Guid Id {get; set;}
    public Guid StudentId {get; set;}
}
```

Now, assume that our orchestrator service StudentOrchestrationService is ensuring every new student that gets registered will need to have a library card, so our logic may look as follows:

```
public async ValueTask<Student> RegisterStudentAsync(Student student)
{
    Student registeredStudent =
        await this.studentProcessingService.RegisterStudentAsync(student);

    await AssignStudentLibraryCardAsync(student);

    return registeredStudent;
}

private async ValueTask<LibraryCard> AssignStudentLibraryCardAsync(Student student)
{
    LibraryCard studentLibraryCard = MapToLibraryCard(student);

    return await this.libraryCardProcessingService.AddLibraryCardAsync(studentLibraryCard);
}

private LibraryCard MapToLibraryCard(Student student)
{
    return new LibraryCard
    {
        Id = Guid.NewGuid(),
        StudentId = student.Id
    };
}
```

As you can see above, a valid student id is required to ensure a successful mapping to a `LibraryCard` - and since the mapping is the orchestrator's responsibility, we are required to ensure that the input student and its id is in good shape before proceeding with the orchestration process.

2.1 Foundation Services (Broker-Neighboring)
2.1.0 Introduction

Foundation services are the first point of contact between your business logic and the brokers.

In general, the broker-neighboring services are a hybrid of business logic and an abstraction layer for the processing operations where the higher-order business logic happens, which we will talk about further when we start exploring the processing services in the next section.

Broker-neighboring services main responsibility is to ensure the incoming and outgoing data through the system is validated and vetted structurally, logically and externally.

You can also think of broker-neighboring services as a layer of validation on top of the primitive operations the brokers already offer.

For instance, if a storage broker is offering `InsertStudentAsync(Student student)` as a method, then the broker-neighboring service will offer something as follows:

```
public async ValueTask<Student> AddStudentAsync(Student student)
{
    ValidateStudent(student);

    return await this.storageBroker.InsertStudentAsync(student);
}
```

This makes broker-neighboring services nothing more than an extra layer of validation on top of the existing primitive operations brokers already offer.

2.1.1 On The Map

The broker-neighboring services reside between your brokers and the rest of your application, on the left side higher-order business logic processing services, orchestration, coordination, aggregation or management services may live, or just simply a controller, a UI component or any other data exposure technology.

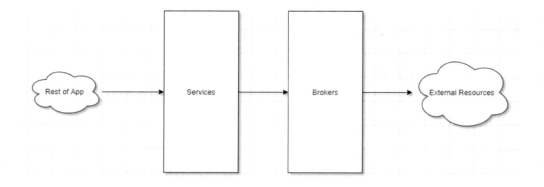

2.1.2 Characteristics

Foundation or Broker-Neighboring services in general have very specific characteristics that strictly govern their development and integration.

Foundation services in general focus more on validations than anything else - simply because that's their purpose, to ensure all incoming and outgoing data through the system is in a good state for the system to process it safely without any issues.

Here's the characteristics and rules that govern broker-neighboring services:

2.1.2.0 Pure-Primitive

Broker-neighboring services are not allowed to combine multiple primitive operations to achieve a higher-order business logic operation.

For instance, broker-neighboring services cannot offer an *upsert* function, to combine a `Select` operations with an `Update` or `Insert` operations based on the outcome to ensure an entity exists and is up to date in any storage.

But they offer a validation and exception handling (and mapping) wrapper around the dependency calls, here's an example:

```
public ValueTask<Student> AddStudentAsync(Student student) =>
TryCatch(async () =>
{
  ValidateStudent(student);

  return await this.storageBroker.InsertStudentAsync(student);
});
```

In the above method, you can see `ValidateStudent` function call preceded by a `TryCatch` block. The `TryCatch` block is what I call Exception Noise Cancellation pattern, which we will discuss soon in this very section.

But the validation function ensures each and every property in the incoming data is validated before passing it forward to the primitive broker operation, which is the `InsertStudentAsync` in this very instance.

2.1.2.1 Single Entity Integration

Services strongly ensure the single responsibility principle is implemented by not integrating with any other entity brokers except for the one that it supports.

This rule doesn't necessarily apply to support brokers like `DateTimeBroker` or `LoggingBroker` since they don't specifically target any particular business entity and they are almost generic across the entire system.

For instance, a `StudentService` may integrate with a `StorageBroker` as long as it only targets only the functionality offered by the partial class in the `StorageBroker.Students.cs` file.

Foundation services should not integrate with more than one entity broker of any kind simply because it will increase the complexity of validation and orchestration which goes beyond the main purpose of the service which is just simply validation. We push this responsibility further to the orchestration-type services to handle it.

2.1.2.2 Business Language

Broker-neighboring services speak primitive business language for their operations. For instance, while a Broker may provide a method with the name `InsertStudentAsync` - the equivelant of that on the service layer would be `AddStudentAsync`.

In general, most of the CRUD operations shall be converted from a storage lanaugage to a business language, and the same goes for non-storage operations such as Queues, for instance we say `PostQueueMessage` but on the business layer we shall say `EnqueueMessage`.

Since the CRUD operations the most common ones in every system, our mapping to these CRUD operations would be as follows:

Brokers	Services
Insert	Add
Select	Retrieve
Update	Modify
Delete	Remove

As we move forward towards higher-order business logic services, the language of the methods beings used will lean more towards a business language rather than a technology language as we will see in the upcoming sections.

2.1.3 Responsibilities

Broker-neighboring services play three very important roles in any system. The first role is to abstract away native broker operations from the rest of the system. Irregardless of whether a broker is a communication between a local or external storage or an API - broker-neighboring services will always have the same contract/verbiage to expose to upper stream services such as processing, orchestration or simply exposers like controllers or UI components. The second and most important role is to offer a layer of validation on top of the existing primitive operations a broker already offers to ensure incoming and outgoing data is valid to be processed or persisted by the system. The third role is to play the role of a mapper of all other native models and contracts that may be needed to completed any given operation while interfacing with a broker. Foundation services are the last point of abstraction between the core business logic of any system and the rest of the world, let's discuss these roles in detail.

2.1.3.0 Abstraction

The first and most important responsibility for foundation/broker-neighboring services is to ensure a level of abstraction exists between the brokers and the rest of your system. This abstraction is necessary to ensure the pure business logic layer in any system is verbally and functionally agnostic to whichever dependencies the system is relying on to communicate with the outside world.

Let's visualize a concrete example of the above principle. Let's assume we have a `StudentProcessingService` which implements an `UpsertStudent Async` functionality. Somewhere in that implementation there will be a dependency on `AddStudentAsync` which is exposed and implemented by some `StudentService` as a foundation service. Take a look at this snippet:

```
public async ValueTask<Student> UpsertStudentAsync(Student student)
{
   ...

   return await this.studentService.AddStudentAsync(student);
}
```

The contract between a processing or an orchestration service and a foundation service will always be the same irregardless of what type of implementation or what type of brokers the foundation service is using. For example, `AddStudentAsync` could be a call to a database or an API endpoint or simply putting a message on a queue. It all doesn't impact in any way, shape or form the upstream processing service implementation. here's an example of three different implementations of a foundation service that wouldn't change anything in the implementation of it's upstream services:

With a storage broker:

```
public async ValueTask<Student> AddStudentAsync(Student student)
{
  ...
  return await this.storageBroker.InsertStudentAsync(student);
}
```

Or with a queue broker:

```
public async ValueTask<Student> AddStudentAsync(Student student)
{
  ...
  return await this.queueBroker.EnqueueStudentAsync(student);
}
```

or with an API broker:

```
public async ValueTask<Student> AddStudentAsync(Student student)
{
  ...
  return await this.apiBroker.PostStudentAsync(student);
}
```

here's a visualization of that concept:

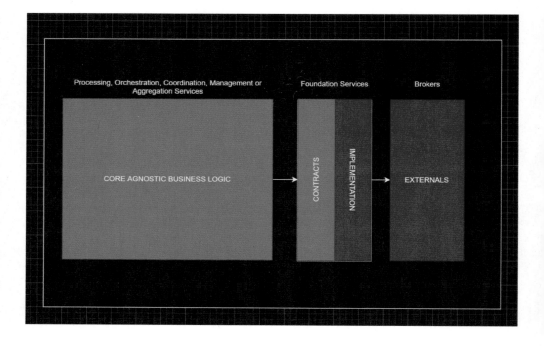

In all of these above cases, the underlying implementation may change, but the exposed contract will always stay the same for the rest of the system. We will discuss in later chapters how the core, agnostic and abstreact business logic of your system starts with Processing services and ends with Management or Aggregation services.

2.1.3.0.1 Implementation

Let's talk about a real-life example of implementing a simple Add function in a foundation service. Let's assume we have the following contract for our StudentService:

```
public IStudentService
{
    ValueTask<Student> AddStudentAsync(Student student);
}
```

For starters, let's go ahead and write a failing test for our service as follows:

```
public async Task ShouldAddStudentAsync()
{
    // given
    Student randomStudent = CreateRandomStudent();
    Student inputStudent = randomStudent;
    Student storageStudent = inputStudent;
    Student expectedStudent = storageStudent.DeepClone();

    this.storageBrokerMock.Setup(broker =>
        broker.InsertStudentAsync(inputStudent))
            .ReturnsAsync(storageStudent);

    // when
    Student actualStudent =
        await this.studentService.AddStudentAsync(inputStudent);

    // then
    actualStudent.Should().BeEquivalentTo(expectedStudent);

    this.storageBroker.Verify(broker =>
        broker.InsertStudentAsync(inputStudent),
        Times.Once);

    this.storageBroker.VerifyNoOtherCalls();
    this.loggingBroker.VerifyNoOtherCalls();
}
```

In the above test, we defined four variables with the same value. Each
variable contains a name that best fits the context it will be used in. For
instance, inputStudent best fits in the input parameter position, while sto
rageStudent best first what gets returned from the storage broker after a
student is persisted sucessfully.

You will also notice that we deep cloned the expectedStudent variable to
ensure no modifications have happened to the originally passed in student.
For instance, assume an input student value has changed for any of it's
attributes internally within the AddStudentAsync function. That change
won't trigger a failing test unless we dereference the expectedStudent
variable from the input and returned variables.

We mock the response from the storage broker and execute our subject of
test AddStudentAsync then we verify the returned student value actualSt
udent matches the expected value expectedStudent regardless of the
reference.

Finally, we verify all calls are done properly and no additional calls has been
made to any of the service dependencies.

Let's make that test pass by writing in an implementation that only satisfies
the requirements of the aforementioned test:

```
public async ValueTask<Student> AddStudentAsync(Student student) =>
    await this.storageBroker.InsertStudentAsync(student);
```

This simple implementation should make our test pass sucessfully. It's
important to understand that any implementation should be only enough to
pass the failing tests. Nothing more and nothing less.

2.1.3.1 Validation

Foundation services are required to ensure incoming and outgoing data from and to the system are in a good state - they play the role of a gatekeeper between the system and the outside world to ensure the data that goes through is structurally, logically and externally valid before performing any further operations by upstream services. The order of validations here is very intentional. Structural validations are the cheapest of all three types. They ensure a particular attribute or piece of data in general doesn't have a default value if it's required. the opposite of that is the logical validations, where attributes are compared to other attributes with the same entity or any other. Additional logical validations can also include a comparison with a constant value like comparing a student enrollment age to be no less than 5 years of age. Both strucural and logical validations come before the external. As we said, it's simply because we don't want to pay the cost of communicating with an external resource including latency tax if our request is not in a good shape first. For instance, we shouldn't try to post some `Stud ent` object to an external API if the object is `null`. Or if the `Student` model is invalid structurally or logically.

For all types of validations, it's important to understand that some validations are circuit-breaking or requiring an immediate exit from the current flow by throwing an exception or returning a value in some cases. And some other validations are continuous. Let's talk about these two sub categories of validations first.

2.1.3.1.0 Circuit-Breaking Validations

Circuit-breaking validations require an immediate exit from the current flow. For instance, if an object being passed into a function is `null` - there will be no further operations required at that level other than exiting the current flow by throwing an exception or returning a value of some type. Here's an example: In some validation scenario, assume that our `AddStudent` function has a student of value `null` passed into it as follows:

```
Student noStudent = null;
await this.studentService.AddStudentAsync(noStudent);
```

Our `AddStudentAsync` function in this scenario is now required to validate whether the passed in parameter is `null` or not before going any further with any other type of validations or the business logic itself. Something like this:

```
public Student AddStudentAsync(Student student) =>
TryCatch(async () =>
{
    ValidateStudent(student);

    return await this.storageBroker.InsertStudentAsync(student);
});
```

The statement in focus here is `ValidateStudent` function and what it does.
Here's an example of how that routine would be implemented:

```
private void ValidateStudent(Student student)
{
    if(student is null)
    {
        throw new NullStudentException();
    }
}
```

In the function above, we decided to throw the exception immediately instead
of going in further. That's an example of circuit-breaking validation type.

But with validations, circuit-breaking isn't always the wise thing to do.
Sometimes we want to collect all the issues within a particular request before
sending the error report back to the request submitter. Let's talk about that
in this next section.

2.1.3.1.1 Continuous Validations

Continuous validations are the opposite of circuit-breaking validations. They
don't stop the flow of validations but they definitely stop the flow of logic. In
other words, continuous validations ensure no business logic will be executed
but they also ensure other validations of the same type can continue to
execute before breaking the circuit. Let's materialize this theory with an
example: Assume our student model looks like this:

```
public class Student
{
    public Guid Id {get; set;}
    public string Name {get; set;}
}
```

Assuming that the passed in `Student` model is not null, but it has default
values across the board for all it's properties. We want to collect all these
issues for however many attributes/properties this object has and return a
full report back to the requestor. Here's how to do it.

2.1.3.1.1.0 Upsertable Exceptions

A problem of that type requires a special type of exceptions that allow collecting all errors in it's `Data` property. Every native exception out there will contain the `Data` property which is basically a dictionary for a key/value pairs for collecting more information about the issues that caused that exception to occur. The issue with these native exceptions is that they don't have native support for upsertion. Being able to append to an existing list of values against a particular key at any point of time. Here's a native implementation of upserting values in some given dictionary:

```
var someException = new Exception();

if(someException.Data.Contains(someKey))
{
    (someException.Data[someKey] as List<string>)?.Add(someValue);
}
else
{
    someException.Data.Add(someKey, new List<string>{ someValue });
}
```

This implementation can be quite daunting for engineers to think about and test in their service-level implementation. It felt more appropriate to introduce a simple library `Xeptions` to simplify the above implementation into something as simple as:

```
var someException = new Xeption();
someException.UpsertData(someKey, someValue);
```

Now that we have this library to utilize, the concern of implementing upsertable exceptions has been addressed. This means that we have what it takes to collect our validation errors. But that's not good enough if we don't have a mechanism to break the circuit when we believe that the time is right to do so. We can simply use the native offerings to implement the circuit-breaking directly as follows:

```
if(someException.Data.Count > 0)
{
    throw someException;
}
```

And while this can be easily baked into any existing implementation. It still didn't contribute much to overall look-n-feel of the code. Therefore I have decided to make it a part of the `Xeptions` library to be simplified to the following:

```
someException.ThrowIfContainsErrors();
```

That would make our custom validations look something like this:

```
public class InvalidStudentException : Xeption
{
    public InvalidStudentException()
        : base ("Student is invalid. Please fix the errors and try again.")
    { }
}
```

But with continuous validations, the process of collecting these errors conveys more than just a special exception implementation. Let's talk about that in the next section.

2.1.3.1.1.1 Dynamic Rules

A non-circuit-breaking or continuous validation process will require the ability to pass in dynamic rules at any count or capacity to add these validation errors. A validation rule is a dynamic structure that reports whether the rule has been violated for its condition; and also the error message that should be reported to the end user to help them fix that issue.

In a scenario where we want to ensure any given Id is valid, a dynamic continuous validation rule would look something like this:

```
private static dynamic IsInvalid(Guid id) => new
{
    Condition = id == Guid.Empty,
    Message = "Id is required"
};
```

Now our Rule doesn't just report whether a particular attribute is invalid or not. It also has a meaningful human-readable message that helps the consumer of the service understand what makes that very attribute invalid.

It's really important to point out the language engineers must use for validation messages. It will all depend on the potential consumers of your system. A non-engineer will not understand a message such as Text cannot be null, empty or whitespace - null as a term isn't something that is very commonly used. Engineers must work closely with their meatware (The people using the system) to ensure the language makes sense to them.

Dynamic rules by design will allow engineers to modify both their inputs and outputs without breaking any existing functionality as long as null values are considered across the board. Here's another manifestation of a Dynamic Validation Rule:

```
private static dynamic IsNotSame(
    Guid firstId,
    Guid secondId,
    string secondIdName) => new
{
    Condition = firstId != secondId,
    Message = $"Id is not the same as {secondIdName}.",
    HelpLink = "/help/code1234"
};
```

Our dynamic rule now can offer more input parameters and more helpful information in terms of more detailed exception message with links to helpful documentation sites or references for error codes.

2.1.3.1.1.2 Rules & Validations Collector

Now that have the advanced exceptions and the dynamic validation rules. It's time to put it all together in terms of accepting infinite number of validation rules, examining their condition results and finally break the circuit when all the continuous validations are done. here's how to do that:

```
private void Validate(params (dynamic Rule, string Parameter)[] validations)
{
    var invalidStudentException = new InvalidStudentException();

    foreach((dynamic rule, string parameter) in validations)
    {
        if(rule.Condition)
        {
            invalidStudentException.UpsertData(parameter, rule.Message);
        }
    }

    invalidStudentException.ThrowIfContainsErrors();
}
```

The above function now will take any number of validation rules, and the parameters the rule is running against then examine the conditions and upsert the report of errors. This is how we can use the method above:

```
private void ValidateStudent(Student student)
{
    Validate(
        (Rule: IsInvalid(student.Id), Parameter: nameof(Student.Id)),
        (Rule: IsInvalid(student.Name), Parameter: nameof(Student.name)),
        (Rule: IsInvalid(student.Grade), Parameter: nameof(Student.Grade))
    );
}
```

This simplification of writing the rules and validations is the ultimate goal of continuing to provide value to the end users while making the process of engineering the solution pleasant to the engineers themselves.

Now, let's dive deeper into the types of validations that our systems can offer and how to handle them.

2.1.3.1.2 Structural Validations

Validations are three different layers. the first of these layers is the structural validations. to ensure certain properties on any given model or a primitive type are not in an invalid structural state.

For instance, a property of type `String` should not be empty, `null` or white space. another example would be for an input parameter of an `int` type, it should not be at it's `default` state which is `0` when trying to enter an age for instance.

The structural validations ensure the data is in a good shape before moving forward with any further validations - for instance, we can't possibly validate a student has the minimum number of characters (which is a logical validation) in their names if their first name is structurally invalid structurally by being null, empty or whitespace.

Structural validations play the role of identifying the *required* properties on any given model, and while a lot of technologies offer the validation annotations, plugins or libraries to globally enforce data validation rules, I choose to perform the validation programmatically and manually to gain more control of what would be required and what wouldn't in a TDD fashion.

The issue with some of the current implementations on structural and logical validations on data models is that it can be very easily changed under the radar without any unit tests firing any alarms. Check this example for instance:

```
public Student
{
   [Required]
   public string Name {get; set;}
}
```

The above example can be very enticing at a glance from an engineering standpoint. All you have to do is decorate your model attribute with a magical annotation and then all of the sudden your data is being validated.

The problem here is that this pattern combines two different responsibilities or more together all in the same model. Models are supposed to be just a representation of objects in reality - nothing more and nothing less. Some engineers call them anemic models which focuses the responsibility of every single model to only represent the attributes of the real world object it's trying to simulate without any additional details.

But the annotated models now try to inject business logic into their very definitions. This business logic may or may not be needed across all services, brokers or exposing components that uses them.

Structural validations on models may seem like extra work that can be avoided with magical decorations. But in the case of trying to diverge slightly from these validations into a more customized validations, now you will see a new anti-pattern emerge like custom annotations that may or may not be detectable through unit tests.

Let's talk about how to test a structural validation routine:

2.1.3.1.2.0 Testing Structural Validations

Because I truly believe in the importance of TDD, I am going to start showing the implementation of structural validations by writing a failing test for it first.

Let's assume we have a student model, with the following details:

```
public class Student
{
    public Guid Id {get; set;}
}
```

We want to validate that the student Id is not a structurally invalid Id - such as an empty `Guid` - therefore we would write a unit test in the following fashion:

```
[Fact]
public async void ShouldThrowValidationExceptionOnRegisterWhenIdIsInvalidAndLogItAsync()
{
    // given
    Student randomStudent = CreateRandomStudent();
    Student inputStudent = randomStudent;
    inputStudent.Id = Guid.Empty;

    var invalidStudentException = new InvalidStudentException();

    invalidStudentException.AddData(
        key: nameof(Student.Id),
        value: "Id is required"
    );

    var expectedStudentValidationException =
        new StudentValidationException(invalidStudentException);

    // when
    ValueTask<Student> registerStudentTask =
        this.studentService.RegisterStudentAsync(inputStudent);

    StudentValidationException actualStudentValidationException =
        await Assert.ThrowsAsync<StudentValidationException>(
            registerStudentTask.AsTask);

    // then
    actualStudentValidationException.Should().BeEquivalentTo(
        expectedStudentValidationException);

    this.loggingBrokerMock.Verify(broker =>
        broker.LogError(It.Is(SameExceptionAs(
            expectedStudentValidationException))),
            Times.Once);

    this.storageBrokerMock.Verify(broker =>
        broker.InsertStudentAsync(It.IsAny<Student>()),
            Times.Never);

    this.dateTimeBrokerMock.VerifyNoOtherCalls();
    this.loggingBrokerMock.VerifyNoOtherCalls();
    this.storageBrokerMock.VerifyNoOtherCalls();
}
```

In the above test, we created a random student object then assigned the an invalid Id value of `Guid.Empty` to the student `Id`.

When the structural validation logic in our foundation service examines the `Id` property, it should throw an exception property describing the issue of validation in our student model. in this case we throw `InvalidStudentException`.

The exception is required to briefly describe the whats, wheres and whys of the validation operation. in our case here the what would be the validation issue occurring, the where would be the Student service and the why would be the property value.

Here's how an `InvalidStudentException` would look like:

```
public class InvalidStudentException : Xeption
{
    public InvalidStudentException()
      :base ("Student is invalid. Please fix the errors and try again.")
    { }
}
```

The above unit test however, requires our `InvalidStudentException` to be wrapped up in a more generic system-level exception, which is `StudentVali dationException` - these exceptions is what I call outer-exceptions, they encapsulate all the different situations of validations regardless of their category and communicates the error to upstream services or controllers so they can map that to the proper error code to the consumer of these services.

Our `StudentValidationException` would be implemented as follows:

```
public class StudentValidationException : Exception
{
    public StudentValidationException(Exception innerException)
      : base("Student validation error occurred, please check your input and then try again.", innerException) { }
}
```

The message in the outer-validation above indicates that the issue is in the input, and therefore it requires the input submitter to try again as there are no actions required from the system side to be adjusted.

2.1.3.1.2.1 Implementing Structural Validations

Now, let's look at the other side of the validation process, which is the implementation. Structural validations always come before each and every other type of validations. That's simply because structural validations are the cheapest from an execution and asymptotic time perspective. For instance, It's much cheaper to validation an `Id` is invalid structurally, than sending an API call across to get the exact same answer plus the cost of latency. This all adds up when multi-million requests per second start flowing in. Structural and logical validations in general live in their own partial class to run these validations, for instance, if our service is called `StudentService.cs` then a new file should be created with the name `StudentService.Validations.cs` to encapsulate and visually abstract away the validation rules to ensure clean data are coming in and going out. Here's how an Id validation would look like:

StudentService.Validations.cs

```csharp
private void ValidateStudent(Student student)
{
    Validate((Rule: IsInvalid(student.Id), Parameter: nameof(Student.Id)));
}

private static dynamic IsInvalid(Guid id) => new
{
    Condition = id == Guid.Empty,
    Message = "Id is required"
};

private void Validate(params (dynamic Rule, string Parameter)[] validations)
{
    var invalidStudentException = new InvalidStudentException();

    foreach((dynamic rule, string parameter) in validations)
    {
        if(rule.Condition)
        {
            invalidStudentException.UpsertData(parameter, rule.Message);
        }
    }

    invalidStudentException.ThrowIfContainsErrors();
}
```

We have implemented a method to validate the entire student object, with a compilation of all the rules we need to setup to validate structurally and logically the student input object. The most important part to notice about the above code snippet is to ensure the encapsulation of any finer details further away from the main goal of a particular method.

That's the reason why we decided to implement a private static method `IsInvalid` to abstract away the details of what determines a property of type `Guid` is invalid or not. And as we move further in the implementation, we are going to have to implement multiple overloads of the same method to validate other value types structurally and logically.

The purpose of the `ValidateStudent` method is to simply set up the rules and take an action by throwing an exception if any of these rules are violated. There's always an opportunity to aggregate the violation errors rather than throwing too early at the first sign of structural or logical validation issue to be detected.

Now, with the implementation above, we need to call that method to structurally and logically validate our input. Let's make that call in our `RegisterStudentAsync` method as follows:

StudentService.cs

```csharp
public ValueTask<Student> RegisterStudentAsync(Student student) =>
TryCatch(async () =>
{
    ValidateStudent(student);

    return await this.storageBroker.InsertStudentAsync(student);
});
```

At a glance, you will notice that our method here doesn't necessarily handle any type of exceptions at the logic level. That's because all the exception noise is also abstracted away in a method called `TryCatch`.

`TryCatch` is a concept I invented to allow engineers to focus on what matters that most based on which aspect of the service that are looking at without having to take any shortcuts with the exception handling to make the code a bit more readable.

`TryCatch` methods in general live in another partial class, and an entirely new file called `StudentService.Exceptions.cs` - which is where all exception handling and error reporting happens as I will show you in the following example.

Let's take a look at what a `TryCatch` method looks like:

StudentService.Exceptions.cs

```
private delegate ValueTask<Student> ReturningStudentFunction();

private async ValueTask<Student> TryCatch(ReturningStudentFunction returningStudentFunction)
{
  try
  {
    return await returningStudentFunction();
  }
  catch (InvalidStudentException invalidStudentInputException)
  {
    throw CreateAndLogValidationException(invalidStudentInputException);
  }
}

private StudentValidationException CreateAndLogValidationException(Exception exception)
{
  var studentValidationException = new StudentValidationException(exception);
  this.loggingBroker.LogError(studentValidationException);

  return studentValidationException;
}
```

The `TryCatch` exception noise-cancellation pattern beautifully takes in any function that returns a particular type as a delegate and handles any thrown exceptions off of that function or it's dependencies.

The main responsibility of a `TryCatch` function is to wrap up a service inner exceptions with outer exceptions to ease-up the reaction of external consumers of that service into only one of the three categories, which are Service Exceptions, Validations Exceptions and Dependency Exceptions. there are sub-types to these exceptions such as Dependency Validation Exceptions but these usually fall under the Validation Exception category as we will discuss in upcoming sections of The Standard.

In a `TryCatch` method, we can add as many inner and external exceptions as we want and map them into local exceptions for upstream services not to have a strong dependency on any particular libraries or external resource models, which we will talk about in detail when we move on to the Mapping responsibility of broker-neighboring (foundation) services.

2.1.3.1.3 Logical Validations

Logical validations are the second in order to structural validations. their main responsibility by definition is to logically validate whether a structurally valid piece of data is logically valid. For instance, a date of birth for a student could be structurally valid by having a value of 1/1/1800 but logically, a student that is over 200 years of age is an impossibility.

The most common logical validations are validations for audit fields such as `CreatedBy` and `UpdatedBy` - it's logically impossible that a new record can be inserted with two different values for the authors of that new record - simply because data can only be inserted by one person at a time.

Let's talk about how we can test-drive and implement logical validations:

2.1.3.1.3.0 Testing Logical Validations

In the common case of testing logical validations for audit fields, we want to throw a validation exception that the `UpdatedBy` value is invalid simply because it doesn't match the `CreatedBy` field.

Let's assume our Student model looks as follows:

```
public class Student {
    Guid CreatedBy {get; set;}
    Guid UpdatedBy {get; set;}
}
```

Our test to validate these values logically would be as follows:

```
[Fact]
public async Task ShouldThrowValidationExceptionOnRegisterIfUpdatedByNotSameAsCreatedByAndLogItAsync()
{
    // given
    Student randomStudent = CreateRandomStudent();
    Student inputStudent = randomStudent;
    inputStudent.UpdatedBy = Guid.NewGuid();

    var invalidStudentException = new InvalidStudentException();

    invalidStudentException.AddData(
        key: nameof(Student.UpdatedBy),
        value: $"Id is not the same as {nameof(Student.CreatedBy)}.");

    var expectedStudentValidationException =
        new StudentValidationException(invalidStudentException);

    // when
    ValueTask<Student> registerStudentTask =
        this.studentService.RegisterStudentAsync(inputStudent);

    StudentValidationException actualStudentValidationException =
        await Assert.ThrowsAsync<StudentValidationException>(
            registerStudentTask.AsTask);

    // then
    actualStudentValidationException.Should().BeEquivalentTo(
        expectedStudentValidationException);

    this.loggingBrokerMock.Verify(broker =>
        broker.LogError(It.Is(SameExceptionAs(
            expectedStudentValidationException))),
            Times.Once);

    this.storageBrokerMock.Verify(broker =>
        broker.InsertStudentAsync(It.IsAny<Student>()),
            Times.Never);

    this.loggingBrokerMock.VerifyNoOtherCalls();
    this.dateTimeBrokerMock.VerifyNoOtherCalls();
    this.storageBrokerMock.VerifyNoOtherCalls();
}
```

In the above test, we have changed the value of the `UpdatedBy` field to
ensure it completely differs from the `CreatedBy` field - now we expect an `In
validStudentException` with the `CreatedBy` to be the reason for this
validation exception to occur.

Let's go ahead an write an implementation for this failing test.

2.1.3.1.3.1 Implementing Logical Validations

Just like we did in the structural validations section, we are going to add
more rules to our validation `switch case` as follows:

StudentService.Validations.cs

```csharp
private void ValidateStudent(Student student)
{
  Validate(
    (Rule: IsNotSame(
       firstId: student.UpdatedBy,
       secondId: student.CreatedBy,
       secondIdName: nameof(student.CreatedBy)),
     Parameter: nameof(Student.UpdatedBy))
  );
}

private static dynamic IsNotSame(
  Guid firstId,
  Guid secondId,
  string secondIdName) => new
  {
    Condition = firstId != secondId,
    Message = $"Id is not the same as {secondIdName}."
  };

private void Validate(params (dyanamic Rule, string Parameter)[] validations)
{
  var invalidStudentException = new Exception();

  foreach((dynamic rule, string parameter) in validations)
  {
    if(rule.Condition)
    {
      invalidStudentException.UpsertData(
        key: parameter,
        value: rule.Message);
    }
  }
}
```

Everything else in both `StudentService.cs` and `StudentService.Except ions.cs` continues to be exactly the same as we've done above in the structural validations.

Logical validations exceptions, just like any other exceptions that may occur are usually non-critical. However, it all depends on your business case to determine whether a particular logical, structural or even a dependency validation are critical or not, this is when you might need to create a special class of exceptions, something like `InvalidStudentCriticalException` then log it accordingly.

2.1.3.1.4 External Validations

The last type of validations that are usually performed by foundation services is external validations. I define external validations as any form of validation that requires calling an external resource to validate whether a foundation service should proceed with processing incoming data or halt with an exception.

A good example of dependency validations is when we call a broker to retrieve a particular entity by it's id. If the entity returned is not found, or the API broker returns a `NotFound` error - the foundation service is then required to wrap that error in a `ValidationException` and halts all following processes.

External validation exceptions can occur if the returned value did not match the expectation, such as an empty list returned from an API call when trying to insert a new coach of a team - if there is no team members, there can be no coach for instance. The foundation service in this case will be required to raise a local exception to explain the issue, something like `NoTeamMembersF oundException` or something of that nature.

Let's write a failing test for an external validation example:

2.1.3.1.4.0 Testing External Validations

Let's assume we are trying to retrieve a student with an `Id` that doesn't match any records in the database. Here's how we would go about testing this scenario. First off, let's define a `NotFoundStudentException` model as follows:

```
using Xeption;

public class NotFoundStudentException : Xeption
{
    public NotFoundStudentException(Guid id)
        : base (message: $"Couldn't find a student with id: {id}.")
    {}
}
```

The above model is the localization aspect of handling the issue. Now let's write a failing test as follows:

```
public async Task ShouldThrowValidationExceptionOnRetrieveByIdIfStudentNotFoundAndLogItAsync()
{
    // given
    Guid randomStudentId = Guid.NewGuid();
    Guid inputStudentId = randomStudentId;
    Student noStudent = null;

    var notFoundStudentException =
        new NotFoundStudentException(inputStudentId);

    var expectedStudentValidationException =
        new StudentValidationException(notFoundStudentException);

    this.storageBrokerMock.Setup(broker =>
        broker.SelectStudentByIdAsync(inputStudentId))
            .ReturnsAsync(noStudent);

    // when
    ValueTask<Student> retrieveStudentByIdTask =
        this.studentService.RetrieveStudentByIdAsync(inputStudentId);

    StudentValidationException actualStudentValidationException =
        await Assert.ThrowsAsync<StudentValidationException>(
            retrieveStudentByIdTask.AsTask);

    // then
    actualStudentValidationException.Should().BeEquivalentTo(
        expectedStudentValidationException);

    this.storageBrokerMock.Verify(broker =>
        broker.SelectStudentByIdAsync(inputStudentId),
        Times.Once);

    this.loggingBrokerMock.Verify(broker =>
        broker.LogError(It.Is(SameExceptionAs(
            expectedStudentValidationException))),
            Times.Once);

    this.storageBrokerMock.VerifyNoOtherCalls();
    this.loggingBrokerMock.VerifyNoOtherCalls();
    this.dateTimeBrokerMock.VerifyNotOtherCalls();
}
```

The test above requires us to throw a localized exception as in `NotFoundStu dentException` when the storage broker returns no values for the given `st udentId` and then wrap or categorize this up in `StudentValidationExcep tion`.

We choose to wrap the localized exception in a validation exception and not in a dependency validation exception because the initiation of the error originated from our service not from the external resource. If the external resource is the source of the error we would have to categorize this as a `De pendencyValidationException` which we will discuss shortly.

Now let's get to the implementation part of this section to make our test pass.

2.1.3.1.4.1 Implementing External Validations

In order to implement an external validation we will need to touch on all different aspects of our service. The core logic, the validation and the exception handling aspects are as follows.

First off, let's build a validation function that will throw a `NotFoundStudent Exception` if the passed-in parameter is null.

StudentService.Validations.cs

```
private static void VerifyStudentExists(Student maybeStudent, Guid studentId)
{
    if (maybeStudent is null)
    {
        throw new NotFoundStudentException(studentId);
    }
}
```

This implementation will take care of detecting an issue and issuing a local exception `NotFoundStudentException`. Now let's jump over to the exception handling aspect of our service.

StudentService.Exceptions.cs

```
private async ValueTask<Student> TryCatch(ReturningStudentFunction returningStudentFunction)
{
    try
    {
        return await returningStudentFunction();
    }
    ..
    catch (NotFoundStudentException notFoundStudentException)
    {
        throw CreateAndLogValidationException(notFoundStudentException);
    }
}

private StudentValidationException CreateAndLogValidationException(Exception exception)
{
    var studentValidationException = new StudentValidationException(exception);
    this.loggingBroker.LogError(studentValidationException);

    return studentValidationException;
}
```

The above implementation will take care of categorizing a `NotFoundStuden tException` to `StudentValidationException`. The last part is to put the pieces together as follows.

StudentService.cs

```
public ValueTask<Student> RetrieveStudentByIdAsync(Guid studentId) =>
TryCatch(async () =>
{
  ValidateStudentId(studentId);

  Student maybeStudent =
    await this.storageBroker.SelectStudentByIdAsync(studentId);

  ValidateStudentExists(maybeStudent, studentId);

  return maybeStudent;
});
```

The above implementation will ensure that the id is valid, but more importantly that whatever the `storageBroker` returns will be checked for whether it's an object or `null`. Then issue the exception.

There are situations where attempting to retrieve an entity then finding out that it doesn't exist is not necessarily erroneous. This is where Processing Services come in to leverage a higher-order business logic to deal with this more complex scenario.

2.1.3.1.5 Dependency Validations

Dependency validation exceptions can occur because you called an external resource and it returned an error, or returned a value that warrants raising an error. For instance, an API call might return a `404` code, and that's interpreted as an exception if the input was supposed to correspond to an existing object.

A more common example is when a particular input entity is using the same id as an existing entity in the system. In a relational database world, a duplicate key exception would be thrown. In a RESTful API scneario, programmatically applying the same concept also achieves the same goal for API validations assuming the granularity of the system being called weaken the referential integrity of the overall system data.

There are situations where the faulty response can be expressed in a fashion other than exceptions, but we shall touch on that topic in a more advanced chapters of this Standard.

Let's write a failing test to verify whether we are throwing a `DependencyVa lidationException` if `Student` model already exists in the storage with the storage broker throwing a `DuplicateKeyException` as a native result of the operation.

2.1.3.1.5.0 Testing Dependency Validations

Let's assume our student model uses an `Id` with the type `Guid` as follows:

```
public class Student
{
    public Guid Id {get; set;}
    public string Name {get; set;}
}
```

our unit test to validate a `DependencyValidation` exception would be thrown in a `DuplicateKey` situation would be as follows:

```
[Fact]
public async void ShouldThrowDependencyValidationExceptionOnRegisterIfStudentAlreadyExistsAndLogItAsync()
{
    // given
    Student someStudent = CreateRandomStudent();
    string someMessage = GetRandomMessage();
    var duplicateKeyException = new DuplicateKeyException(exceptionMessage);

    var alreadyExistsStudentException =
        new AlreadyExistsStudentException(duplicateKeyException);

    var expectedStudentDependencyValidationException =
        new StudentDependencyValidationException(alreadyExistsStudentException);

    this.storageBrokerMock.Setup(broker =>
        broker.InsertStudentAsync(It.IsAny<Student>()))
          .ThrowsAsync(duplicateKeyException);

    // when
    ValueTask<Student> registerStudentTask =
        this.studentService.RegisterStudentAsync(inputStudent);

    StudentDependencyValidationException actualStudentDependencyValidationException =
        await Assert.ThrowsAsync<StudentDependencyValidationException>(
            registerStudentTask.AsTask);

    // then
    actualStudentDependencyValidationException.Should().BeEquivalentTo(
        expectedStudentDependencyValidationException);

    this.storageBrokerMock.Verify(broker =>
        broker.InsertStudentAsync(It.IsAny<Student>()),
        Times.Once);

    this.loggingBrokerMock.Verify(broker =>
        broker.LogError(It.Is(SameExceptionAs(
            expectedStudentDependencyValidationException))),
        Times.Once);

    this.storageBrokerMock.VerifyNoOtherCalls();
    this.loggingBrokerMock.VerifyNoOtherCalls();
}
```

In the above test, we validate that we wrap a native `DuplicateKeyExcepti on` in a local model tailored to the specific model case which is the `Already ExistsStudentException` in our example here. then we wrap that again with a generic category exception model which is the `StudentDependencyV alidationException`.

There's a couple of rules that govern the construction of dependency validations, which are as follows:

- Rule 1: If a dependency validation is handling another dependency validation from a downstream service, then the inner exception of the downstream exception should be the same for the dependency validation at the current level.

In other words, if some `StudentService` is throwing a `StudentDependencyValidationException` to an upstream service such as `StudentProcessingService` - then it's important that the `StudentProcessingDependencyValidationException` contain the same inner exception as the `StudentDependencyValidationException`. That's because once these exception are mapped into exposure components, such as API controller or UI components, the original validation message needs to propagate through the system and be presented to the end user no matter where it originated from.

Additionally, maintaining the original inner exception guarantees the ability to communicate different error messages through API endpoints. For instance, `AlreadyExistsStudentException` can be communicated as `Conflict` or `409` on an API controller level - this differs from another dependency validation exception such as `InvalidStudentReferenceException` which would be communicated as `FailedDependency` error or `424`.

- Rule 2: If a dependency validation exception is handling a non-dependency validation exception it should take that exception as it's inner exception and not anything else.

These rules ensures that only the local validation exception is what's being propagated not it's native exception from a storage system or an API or any other external dependency.

Which is the case that we have here with our `AlreadyExistsStudentException` and it's `StudentDependencyValidationException` - the native exception is completely hidden away from sight, and the mapping of that native exception and it's inner message is what's being communicated to the end user. This gives the engineers the power to control what's being communicated from the other end of their system instead of letting the native message (which is subject to change) propagate to the end-users.

2.1.3.0.5.1 Implementing Dependency Validations

Depending on where the validation error originates from, the implementation of dependency validations may or may not contain any business logic. As we previously mentioned, if the error is originating from the external resource (which is the case here) - then all we have to do is just wrap that error in a local exception then categorize it with an external exception under dependency validation.

To ensure the aforementioned test passed, we are going to need few models. For the `AlreadyExistsStudentException` the implementation would be as follows:

```
public class AlreadyExistsStudentException : Exception
{
    public AlreadyExistsStudentException(Exception innerException)
        : base($"Student with the same Id already exists", innerException){ }
}
```

We also need the `StudentDependencyValidationException` which should be as follows:

```
public class StudentDependencyValidationException : Exception
{
    public StudentDependencyValidationException(Exception innerException)
        : base($"Student dependency validation error occurred, please try again.", innerException){ }
}
```

Now, let's go to the implementation side, let's start with the exception handling logic:

StudentService.Exceptions.cs

```
private delegate ValueTask<Student> ReturningStudentFunction();

private async ValueTask<Student> TryCatch(ReturningStudentFunction returningStudentFunction)
{
    try
    {
        return await returningStudentFunction();
    }
    ...
    catch (DuplicateKeyException duplicateKeyException)
    {
        var alreadyExistsStudentException = new AlreadyExistsStudentException(duplicateKeyException);
        throw CreateAndLogDependencyValidationException(alreadyExistsStudentException);
    }
}

...

private StudentDependencyValidationException CreateAndLogDependencyValidationException(Exception exception)
{
    var studentDependencyValidationException = new StudentDependencyValidationException(exception);
    this.loggingBroker.LogError(studentDependencyValidationException);

    return studentDependencyValidationException;
}
```

We created the local inner exception in the catch block of our exception handling process to allow the reusability of our dependency validation exception method for other situations that require that same level of external exceptions.

Everything else stays the same for the referencing of the `TryCatch` method in the `StudentService.cs` file.

2.1.3.2 Mapping

The second responsibility for a foundation service is to play the role of a mapper both ways between local models and non-local models. For instance, if you are leveraging an email service that provides it's own SDKs to integrate with, and your brokers are already wrapping and exposing the APIs for that service, your foundation service is required to map the inputs and outputs of the broker methods into local models. the same situation and more commonly between native non-local exceptions such as the ones we mentioned above with the dependency validation situation, the same aspect applies to just dependency errors or service errors as we will discuss shortly.

2.1.3.2.0 Non-Local Models

Its very common for modern applications to require integration at some point with external services. these services can be local to the overall architecture or distributed system where the application lives, or it can be a 3rd party provider such as some of the popular email services for instance. External services providers invest a lot of effort in developing fluent APIs, SDKs and libraries in every common programming language to make it easy for the engineers to integrate their applications with that 3rd party service. For instance, let's assume a third party email service provider is offering the following API through their SDKs:

```
public interface IEmailServiceProvider
{
    ValueTask<EmailMessage> SendEmailAsync(EmailMessage message);
}
```

Let's consider the model `EmailMessage` is a native model, it comes with the email service provider SDK. your brokers might offer a wrapper around this API by building a contract to abstract away the *functionality* but can't do much with the native models that are passed in or returned out of these functionality. therefore our brokers interface would look something like this:

```
public interface IEmailBroker
{
    ValueTask<EmailMessage> SendEmailMessageAsync(EmailMessage message);
}
```

Then the implementation would something like this:

```
public class EmailBroker : IEmailBroker
{
    public async ValueTask<EmailMessage> SendEmailMessageAsync(EmailMessage message) =>
        await this.emailServiceProvider.SendEmailAsync(message);
}
```

As we said before, the brokers here have done their part of abstraction by pushing away the actual implementation and the dependencies of the native `EmailServiceProvider` away from our foundation serviecs. But that's only 50% of the job, the abstraction isn't quite fully complete yet until there are no tracks of the native `EmailMessage` model. This is where the foundation services come in to do a test-driven operation of mapping between the native non-local models and your application's local models. therefore its very possible to see a mapping function in a foundation service to abstract away the native model from the rest of your business layer services.

Your foundation service then will be required to support a new local model, let's call it `Email`. your local model's property may be identical to the external model `EmailMessage` - especially on a primitive data type level. But the new model would be the one and only contract between your pure business logic layer (processing, orchestration, coordination and management services) and your hybrid logic layer like the foundation services. Here's a code snippet for this operation:

```
public async ValueTask<Email> SendEmailMessageAsync(Email email)
{
    EmailMessage inputEmailMessage = MapToEmailMessage(email);
    EmailMessage sentEmailMessage = await this.emailBroker.SendEmailMessageAsync(inputEmailMessage);

    return MapToEmail(sentEmailMessage);
}
```

Depending on whether the returned message has a status or you would like to return the input message as a sign of a successful operation, both practices are valid in my Standard. It all depends on what makes more sense to the operation you are trying to execute. the code snippet above is an ideal scenario where your code will try to stay true to the value passed in as well as the value returned with all the necessary mapping included.

2.1.3.2.1 Exceptions Mappings

Just like the non-local models, exceptions that are either produced by the external API like the EntityFramework models `DbUpdateException` or any other has to be mapped into local exception models. Handling these non-local exceptions that early before entering the pure-business layer components will prevent any potential tight coupling or dependency on any external model. as it may be very common, that exceptions can be handled differently based on the type of exception and how we want to deal with it internally in the system. For instance, if we are trying to handle a `UserNotFoundException` being thrown from using Microsoft Graph for instance, we might not necessarily want to exit the entire procedure. we might want to continue by adding a user in some other storage for future Graph submittal processing. External APIs should not influence whether your internal operation should halt or not. and therefore handling exceptions on the Foundation layer is the guarantee that this influence is limited within the borders of our external resources handling area of our application and has no impact whatsoever on our core business processes. The following illustration should draw the picture a bit clearer from that perspective:

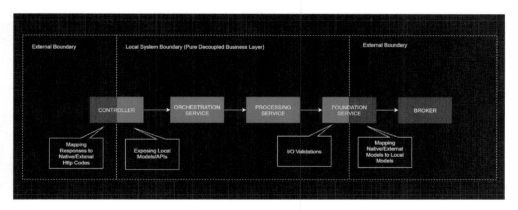

Here's some common scenarios for mapping native or inner local exceptions to outer exceptions:

Exception	Wrap Inner Exception With	Wrap With	Log Level
NullStudentException	-	StudentValidationException	Error
InvalidStudentException	-	StudentValidationException	Error
SqlException	FailedStudentStorageException	StudentDependencyException	Critical
HttpResponseUrlNotFoundException	FailedStudentApiException	StudentDependencyException	Critical
HttpResponseUnauthorizedException	FailedStudentApiException	StudentDependencyException	Critical
NotFoundStudentException	-	StudentValidationException	Error
HttpResponseNotFoundException	NotFoundStudentException	StudentDependencyValidationException	Error
DuplicateKeyException	AlreadyExistsStudentException	StudentDependencyValidationException	Error
HttpResponseConflictException	AlreadyExistsStudentException	StudentDependencyValidationException	Error
ForeignKeyConstraintConflictException	InvalidStudentReferenceException	StudentDependencyValidationException	Error
DbUpdateConcurrencyException	LockedStudentException	StudentDependencyValidationException	Error
DbUpdateException	FailedStudentStorageException	StudentDependencyException	Error
HttpResponseException	FailedStudentApiException	StudentDependencyException	Error
Exception	FailedStudentServiceException	StudentServiceException	Error

[*] Standardizing Validations & Exceptions

[*] Test-Driving Non-Circuit-Breaking Validations

2.2 Processing Services (Higher-Order Business Logic)
2.2.0 Introduction

Processing services are the layer where a higher order of business logic is implemented. They may combine (or orchestrate) two primitive-level functions from their corresponding foundation service to introduce a newer functionality. They may also call one primitive function and change the outcome with a little bit of added business logic. And sometimes processing services are there as a pass-through to introduce balance to the overall architecture.

Processing services are optional, depending on your business need - in a simple CRUD operations API, processing services and all the other categories of services beyond that point will cease to exist as there is no need for a higher order of business logic at that point.

Here's an example of what a Processing service function would look like:

```
public ValueTask<Student> UpsertStudentAsync(Student student) =>
TryCatch(async () =>
{
    ValidateStudent(student);

    IQueryable<Student> allStudents =
        this.studentService.RetrieveAllStudents();

    bool studentExists = allStudents.Any(retrievedStudent =>
        retrievedStudent.Id == student.Id);

    return studentExists switch {
        false => await this.studentService.RegisterStudentAsync(student),
        _ => await this.studentService.ModifyStudentAsync(student.Id)
    };
});
```

Processing services make Foundation services nothing but a layer of validation on top of the existing primitive operations. Which means that Processing services functions are beyond primitive, and they only deal with local models as we will discuss in the upcoming sections.

2.2.1 On The Map

When used, Processing services live between foundation services and the rest of the application. they may not call Entity or Business brokers, but they may call Utility brokers such as logging brokers, time brokers and any other brokers that offer supporting functionality and not specific to any particular business logic. Here's a visual of where processing services are located on the map of our architecture:

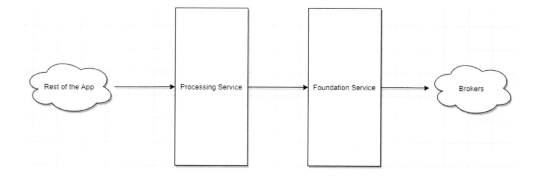

On the right side of a Processing service lies all the non-local models and functionality, whether it's through the brokers, or the models that the foundation service is trying to map into local models. On the left side of Processing services is pure local functionality, models and architecture. Starting from the Processing services themselves, there should be no trace or track of any native or non-local models in the system.

2.2.2 Charachteristics

Processing services in general are combiners of multiple primitive-level functions to produce a higher-order business logic. but they have much more characteristics than just that, let's talk about those here.

2.2.2.0 Language

The language used in processing services defines the level of complexity and the capabilities it offers. Usually, processing services combine two or more primitive operations from the foundation layer to create a new value.

2.2.2.0.0 Functions Language

At a glance, Processing services language change from primitive operations such as `AddStudent` or `RemoveStudent` to `EnsureStudentExists` or `UpsertStudent`. they usually offer a more advanced business-logic operations to support a higher order functionality. Here's some examples for the most common combinations a processing service may offer:

Processing Operation	Primitive Functions
EnsureStudentExistsAsync	RetrieveAllStudents + AddStudentAsync
UpsertStudentAsync	RetrieveStudentById + AddStudentAsync + ModifyStudentAsync
VerifyStudentExists	RetrieveAllStudents
TryRemoveStudentAsync	RetrieveStudentById + RemoveStudentByIdAsync

As you can see, the combination of primitive functions processing services do might also include adding an additional layer of logic on top of the existing primitive operation. For instance, `VerifyStudentExists` takes advantage of the `RetrieveAllStudents` primitive function, and then adds a boolean logic to verify the returned student by and Id from a query actually exists or not before returning a `boolean`.

2.2.2.0.1 Pass-Through

Processing services may borrow some of the terminology a foundation service may use. for instance, in a pass-through scenario, a processing service with be as simple as `AddStudentAsync`. We will discuss the architecture-balancing scenarios later in this chapter. Unlike Foundation services, Processing services are required to have the identifier `Processing` in their names. for instance, we say `StudentProcessingService`.

2.2.2.0.2 Class-Level Language

More importantly Processing services must include the name of the entity that is supported by their corresponding Foundation service. For instance, if a Processing service is dependant on a `TeacherService`, then the Processing service name must be `TeacherProcessingService`.

2.2.2.1 Dependencies

Processing services can only have two types of dependencies. a corresponding Foundation service, or a Utility broker. That's simply because Processing services are nothing but an extra higher-order level of business logic, orchestrated by combined primitive operations on the Foundation level. Processing services can also use Utility brokers such as `TimeBroker` or `LoggingBroker` to support it's reporting aspect. but it shall never interact with an Entity or Business broker.

2.2.2.2 One-Foundation

Processing services can interact with one and only one Foundation service. In fact without a foundation service there can never be a Processing layer. and just like we mentioned above about the language and naming, Processing services take on the exact same entity name as their Foundation dependency. For instance, a processing service that handles higher-order business-logic for students will communicate with nothing but its foundation layer, which would be `StudentService` for instance. That means that processing services will have one and only one service as a dependency in its construction or initiation as follows:

```
public class StudentProcessingService
{
    private readonly IStudentService studentService;

    public StudentProcessingService(IStudentService studentService) =>
        this.studentService = studentService;
}
```

However, processing services may require dependencies on multiple utility brokers such as `DateTimeBroker` or `LoggingBroker` ... etc.

2.2.2.3 Used-Data-Only Validations

Unlike the Foundation layer services, Processing services only validate what it needs from it's input. For instance, if a Processing service is required to validate a student entity exists, and it's input model just happens to be an entire `Student` entity, it will only validate that the entity is not `null` and that the `Id` of that entity is valid. the rest of the entity is out of the concern of the Processing service. Processing services delegate full validations to the layer of services that is concerned with that which is the Foundation layer. here's an example:

```
public ValueTask<Student> UpsertStudentAsync(Student student) =>
TryCatch(async () =>
{
    ValidateStudent(student);

    IQueryable<Student> allStudents =
        this.studentService.RetrieveAllStudents();

    bool isStudentExists = allStudents.Any(retrievedStudent =>
        retrievedStudent.Id == student.Id);

    return isStudentExsits switch {
        false => await this.studentService.RegisterStudentAsync(student),
        _ => await this.studentService.ModifyStudentAsync(student.Id)
    };
});
```

Processing services are also not very concerned about outgoing validations except for what it's going to use within the same routine. For instance, if a Processing service is retrieving a model, and it's going to use this model to be passed to another primitive-level function on the Foundation layer, the Processing service will be required to validate that the retrieved model is valid depending on which attributes of the model it uses. For Pass-through scenarios however, processing services will delegate the outgoing validation to the foundation layer.

2.2.3 Responsibilities

Processing services main responsibility is to provide higher-order business logic. This happens along with the regular signature mapping and various use-only validations which we will discuss in detail in this section.

2.2.3.0 Higher-Order Logic

Higher-order business logic are functions that are above primitive. For instance, `AddStudentAsync` function is a primitive function that does one thing and one thing only. But higher-order logic is when we try to provide a function that changes the outcome of a single primitive function like `Verify StudentExists` which returns a boolean value instead of the entire object of the `Student`, or a combination of multiple primitive functions such as `Ensu reStudentExistsAsync` which is a function that will only add a given `Stud ent` model if and only if the aforementioned object doesn't already exist in storage. here's some examples:

2.2.3.0.0 Shifters

The shifter pattern in a higher order business logic is when the outcome of a particular primitive function is changed from one value to another. Ideally a primitive type such as a `bool` or `int` not a completely different type as that would violate the purity principle. For instance, in a shifter pattern, we want to verify if a student exists or not. We don't really want the entire object, but just whether it exists in a particular system or not. Now, this seems like a case where we only need to interact with one and only one foundation service and we are shifting the value of the outcome to something else. Which should fit perfectly in the realm of the processing services. Here's an example:

```
public ValueTask<bool> VerifyStudentExists(Guid studentId) =>
TryCatch(async () =>
{
    IQueryable<Student> allStudents =
        this.studentService.RetrieveAllStudents();

    ValidateStudents(allStudents);

    return allStudents.Any(student => student.Id == studentId);
});
```

In the snippet above, we provided a higher order business logic, by returning
a boolean value of whether a particular student with a given Id exists in the
system or not. There are cases where your orchestration layer of services
isn't really concerned with all the details of a particular entity but just
knowing whether it exists or not as a part of an upper business logic or what
we call orchestration.

Here's another popular example for processing services shifting pattern:

```
public int RetrieveStudentsCount() =>
TryCatch(() =>
{
    IQueryable<Student> allStudents =
        this.studentService.RetrieveAllStudents();

    ValidateStudents(allStudents);

    return allStudents.Count();
});
```

In the example above, we provided a function to retrieve the count of all
students in a given system. It's up to the designers of the system to determine
whether to interpret a null value retrieved for all students to be an
exception case that was not expected to happen or return a 0; all depending
on how they manage the outcome. In our case here we validate the outgoing
data as much as the incoming, especially if it's going to be used within the
processing function to ensure further failures do not occur for upstream
services.

2.2.3.0.1 Combinations

The combination of multiple primitive functions from the foundation layer to
achieve a higher-order business logic is one of the main responsibilities of a
processing service. As we mentioned before, some of the most popular
examples is for ensuring a particular student model exists as follows:

```
public async ValueTask<Student> EnsureStudentExistsAsync(Student student) =>
TryCatch(async () =>
{
    ValidateStudent(student);

    IQueryable<Student> allStudents =
        this.studentService.RetrieveAllStudents();

    Student maybeStudent = allStudents.FirstOrDefault(retrievedStudent =>
        retrievedStudent.Id == student.Id);

    return maybeStudent switch
    {
        {} => maybeStudent,
        _ => await this.studentService.AddStudentAsync(student)
    };
});
```

In the code snippet above, we combined `RetrieveAll` with `AddAsync` to achieve a higher-order business logic operation. The `EnsureAsync` operation which needs to verify something or entity exists first before trying to persist it. The terminology around these higher-order business logic routines is very important. Its importance lies mainly in controlling the expectations of the outcome and the inner functionality. But it also ensures less cognitive resources from the engineers are required to understand the underlying capabilities of a particular routine. The conventional language used in all of these services also ensures that redundant capability will not be created mistakenly. For instance, an engineering team without any form of standard might create `TryAddStudentAsync` while already having an existing functionality such as `EnsureStudentExistsAsync` which does exactly the same thing. The convention here with the limitation of the size of capabilities a particular service may have ensures redundant work shall never occur in any occassion. There are so many different instances of combinations that can produce a higher-order business logic, for instance we may need to implement a functionality that ensure a student is removed. We use `EnsureStudentRemovedByIdAsync` to combine a `RetrieveById` and a `RemoveById` in the same routine. It all depends on what level of capabilities an upstream service may need to implement such a functionality.

2.2.3.1 Signature Mapping

Although processing services operate fully on local models and local contracts, they are still required to map foundation-level services' models to their own local models. For instance, if a foundation service is throwing `StudentValidationException` then processing services will map that exception to `StudentProcessingDependencyValidationException`. Let's talk about mapping in this section.

2.2.3.1.0 Non-Exception Local Models

In general, processing services are required to map any incoming or outgoing objects with a specific model to its own. But that rule doesn't always apply to non-exception models. For instance, if a `StudentProcessingServi ce` is operating based on a `Student` model, and there's no need for a special model for this service, then the processing service may be permitted to use the exact same model from the foundation layer.

2.2.3.1.1 Exception Models

When it comes to processing services handling exceptions from the foundation layer, it is important to understand that exceptions in our Standard are more expressive in their naming conventions and their role more than any other model. Exceptions here define the what, where and why every single time they are thrown. For instance, an exception that's called `St udentProcessingServiceException` indicates the entity of the exception which is the `Student` entity. Then it indicates the location of the exception which is the `StudentProcessingService`. And lastly it indicates the reason for that exception which is `ServiceException` indicating an internal error to the service that is not a validation or a dependency of nature that happened. Just like the foundation layer, processing services will do the following mapping to occurring exceptions from its dependencies:

Exception	Wrap Inner Exception With	Wrap With	Log Level
StudentDependencyValidationException	Any inner exception	StudentProcessingDependencyValidationException	Error
StudentValidationException	Any inner exception	StudentProcessingDependencyValidationException	Error
StudentDependencyException	-	StudentProcessingDependencyException	Error
StudentServiceException		StudentProcessingDependencyException	Error
Exception		StudentProcessingServiceException	Error

[*] Processing services in Action (Part 1)

[*] Processing services in Action (Part 2)

[*] Processing services in Action (Part 3)

[*] Processing services in Action (Part 4)

2.3 Orchestration Services (Complex Higher Order Logic)
2.3.0 Introduction

Orchestration services are the combinators between multiple foundation or processing services to perform a complex logical operation. Orchestrations main responsibility is to do a multi-entity logical operation and delegate the dependencies of said operation to downstream processing or foundation services. Orchestration services main responsibility is to encapsulate operations that require two or three business entities.

```
public async ValueTask<LibraryCard> CreateStudentLibraryCardAsync(LibraryCard libraryCard) =>
TryCatch(async () =>
{
    ValidateLibraryCard(libraryCard);

    await this.studentProcessingService
        .VerifyEnrolledStudentExistsAsync(libraryCard.StudentId);

    return await this.libraryCardProcessingService.CreateLibraryCardAsync(libraryCard);
});
```

In the above example, the `LibraryCardOrchestrationService` calls both the `StudentProcessingService` and `LibraryCardProcessingService` to perform a complex operation. First, verify the student we are creating a library card for does exist and that they are enrolled. Then second create the library card.

The operation of creating a library card for any given student cannot be performed by simply calling the library card service. That's because the library card service (processing or foundation) does not have access to all the details about the student. Therefore a combination logic here needed to be implemented to ensure a proper flow is in place.

Its important to understand that orchestration services are only required if and only if we need to combine multiple entities operations primitive or higher-order. In some architectures, orchestration services might not even exist. That's simply because some microservices might be simply responsible for applying validation logic and persisting and retrieving data from storage, no more or no less.

2.3.1 On The Map

Orchestration services are one of the core business logic components in any system. They are positioned between single entity services (such as processing or foundation) and advanced logic services such as coordination services, aggregation services or just simply exposers such as controllers, web components or anything else. Here's a high level overview of where orchestration services may live:

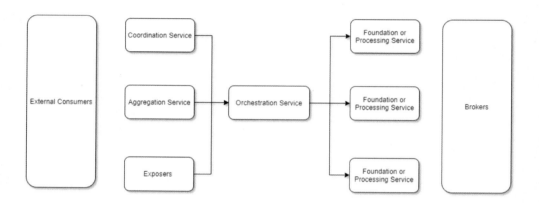

As shown above, orchestration services have quite a few dependencies and consumers. They are the core engine of any software. On the right hand side, you can see the dependencies an orchestration service may have. Since a processing service is optional based on whether a higher-order business logic is needed or not - orchestration services can combine multiple foundation services as well.

The existence of an orchestration service warrants the existence of a processing service. But thats not always the case. There are situations where all orchestration services need to finalize a business flow is to interact with primitive-level functionality.

From a consumer standpoint however, orchestration service could have several consumers. These consumers could range from coordination services (orchestrators of orchestrators) or aggregation services or simply an exposer. Exposers are like controllers, view service, UI components or simply another foundation or processing service in case of putting messages back on a queue - which we will discuss further in our Standard.

2.3.2 Characteristics

In general, orchestration services are concerned with combining single-entity primitive or higher-order business logic operations to execute a successful flow. But you can also think of them as the glue that ties multiple single-entity operations together.

2.3.2.0 Language

Just like processing services, the language used in orchestration services define the level of complexity and the capabilities it offers. Usually, orchestration services combine two or more primitive or higher-order operations from multiple single-entity services to execute a successful operation.

2.3.2.0.0 Functions Language

Orchestration services have a very common charateristic when it comes to the language of it's functions. Orchestration services are wholistic in most of the language of its function, you will see functions such as `NotifyAllAdmins` where the service pulls all users with admin type and then calls a notification service to notify each and every one of them.

It becomes very obvious that orchestration services offer functionality that inches closer and closer to a business language than perimitive technical operation. You may see almost an identical expression in a non-technical business requirement that matches one for one a function name in an orchestration service. The same pattern continues as one goes to higher and more advanced categories of services within that realm of business logic.

2.3.2.0.1 Pass-Through

Orchestration services can also be a pass-through for some operations. For instance, an orchestration service could allow an `AddStudentAsync` to be propagated through the service to unify the source of interactions with the system at the exposers level. In which case, orchestration services will use the very same terminology a processing or a foundation service may use to propagate the operation.

2.3.2.0.2 Class-Level Language

Orchestration services mainly combine multiple operations to support a particular entity. So, if the main entity of support is `Student` and the rest of the entities are just to support an operation mainly targetting a `Student` entity - then the name of the orchestration service would be `StudentOrches trationService`.

This level of enforcement of naming conventions ensures that any orchestration service is staying focused on a single entity responsibility with respect to multiple other supporting entities.

For instance, if creating a library card requires ensuring the student referenced in that library card must be enrolled in a school. Then an orchestration service will then be named after it's main entity which is `Libr aryCard` in this case. Our orchestration service name then would be `Librar yCardOrchestrationService`.

The opposite is also true. If enrolling a student in a school has an accompanying operations such as creating a library card, then in this case a `StudentOrchestrationService` must be created with the main purpose to create a `Student` and then all other related entities once the aforementioned succeeds.

The same idea applies to all exceptions created in an orchestration service such as `StudentOrchestrationValidationException` and `StudentOrch estrationDependencyException` and so on.

2.3.2.1 Dependencies

As we mentioned above, orchestration services might have a bit larger range of types of dependencies unlike processing and foundation services. This is only due the optionality of processing services. Therefore, orchestration services may have dependencies that range from foundation services or processing services and optionally and usually logging or any other utility brokers.

2.3.2.1.0 Dependency Balance (Florance Pattern)

There's a very important rule that govern the consistency and balance of orchestration services which is the 'Florance Pattern'. the rule dictates that any orchestration service may not combine dependencies from different categories of operation.

What that means, is that an orchestration service cannot have a foundation and a processing services combined together. The dependencies has to be either all processings or all foundations. That rule doesn't apply to utility brokers dependencies however.

Here's an example of an unbalanced orchestration service dependencies:

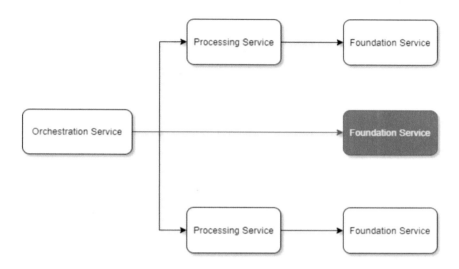

An additional processing service is required to give a pass-through to a lower-level foundation service to balance the architecture - applying 'Florance Pattern' for symmetry would turn our architecture to the following:

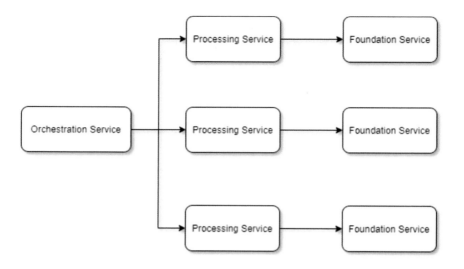

Applying 'Florance Pattern' might be very costly at the beginning as it includes creating an entirely new processing service (or multiple) just to balance the architecture. But its benefits outweighs the effort spent from a maintainability, readability and pluggability perspectives.

2.3.2.1.1 Two-Three

The 'Two-Three' rule is a complexity control rule. This rule dictates that an orchestration service may not have more than three or less than two processing or foundation services to run the orchestration. This rule, however, doesn't apply to utility brokers. And orchestration service may have a `DateTimeBroker` or a `LoggingBroker` without any issues. But an orchestration service may not have an entity broker, such as a `StorageBrok er` or a `QueueBroker` which feeds directly into the core business layer of any service.

The 'Two-Three' rule may require a layer of normalization to the categorical business function that is required to be accomplished. Let's talk about the different mechanisms of normalizing orchestration services.

2.3.2.1.1.0 Full-Normalization

Often times, there are situations where the current architecture of any given orchestration service ends up with one orchestration service that has three dependencies. And a new entity processing or foundation service is required to complete an existing process.

For instance, let's say we have a `StudentContactOrchestrationService` and that service has dependencies that provide primitive-level functionality for `Address`, `Email` and `Phone` for each student. Here's a visualization of that state:

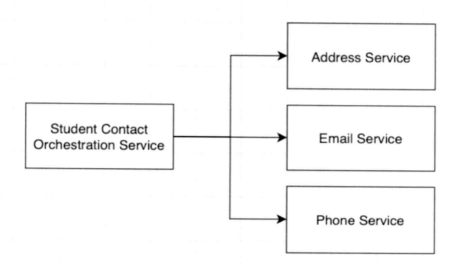

Now, a new requirement comes in to add a student `SocialMedia` to gather more contact information about how to reach a certain student. We can go into full-normalization mode simply by finding the common ground that equally splits the contact information entities. For instance, we can split regular contact information versus digital contact information as in `Address` and `Phone` versus `Email` and `SocialMedia`. this way we split four dependencies into two each for their own orchestration services as follows:

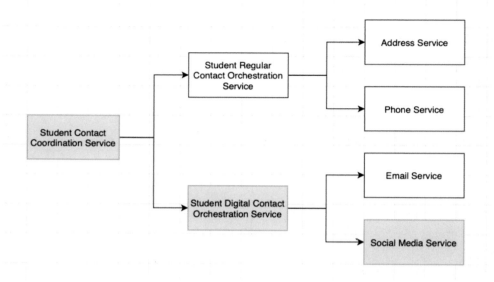

As you can see in the figure above, we modified the existing `StudentContactOrchestrationService` into `StudentRegularContactOrchestrationService`, then we removed one of its dependencies on the `EmailService`.

Additionally, we created a new `StudentDigitalContactOrchestrationService` to have two dependencies on the existing `EmailService` in addition to the new `SocialMediaService`. But now that the normalization is over, we need an advanced order business logic layer, like a coordination service to provide student contact information to upstream consumers.

2.3.2.1.1.1 Semi-Normalization

Normalization isn't always as straightforward as the example above. Especially in situations where a core entity has to exist before creating or writing in additional information towards related entities to that very entity.

For instance, let's say we have a `StudentRegistrationOrchestrationService` which relies on `StudentProcessingService`, `LibraryCardProcessingService` and `BookProcessingService` as follows:

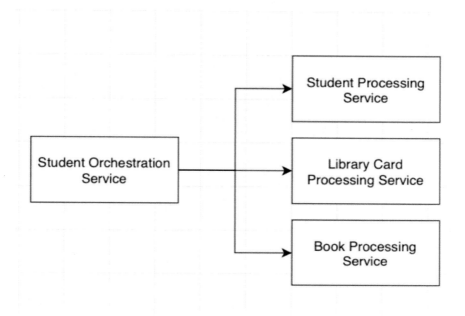

But now, we need a new service to handle students immunization records as `ImmunizationProcessingService`. We need all four services but we already have a `StudentRegistrationOrchestrationService` that has three dependencies. At this point a semi-normalization is required for the re-balancing of the architecture to honor the 'Two-Three' rule and eventually to control the complexity.

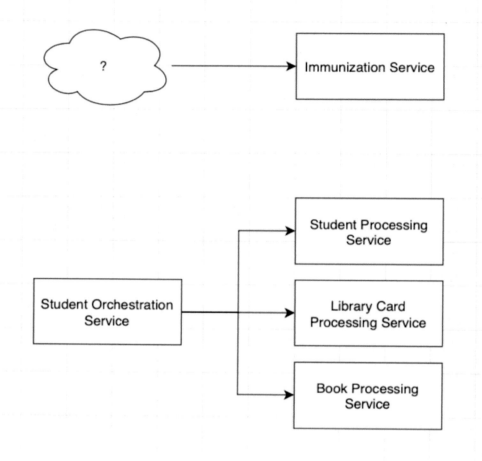

In this case here, a further normalization or a split is required to re-balance the architecture. We need to think conceptually about a common ground between the primitive entities in a student registration process. A student requirements contain identity, health and materials. We can, in this scenario combine LibraryCard and Book under the same orchestration service as books and libraries are somewhat related. So we have StudentLibraryOrc hestrationService and for the other service we would have StudentHeal thOrchestrationService as follows:

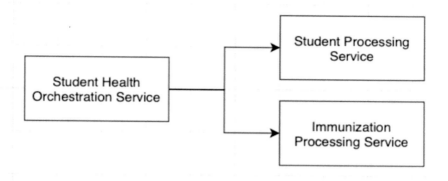

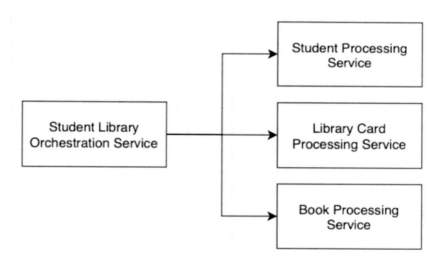

To complete the registration flow with a new model, a coordination service is required to pass-in an advanced business logic to combine all of these entities together. But more importantly, you will notice that each orchestration service now has a redundant dependency of `StudentProcessingService` to ensure no virtual dependency on any other orchestration service create or ensuring a student record exists.

Virtual dependencies are very tricky. it's a hidden connection between two services of any category where one service implicitly assumes that a particular entity will be created and present. Virtual dependencies are very dangerous and threaten the true autonomy of any service. Detecting virtual dependencies at early stage in the design and development process could be a daunting but necessary task to ensure a clean Standardized architecture is in place.

Just like model changes as it may require migrations, and additional logic and validations, a new requirement for an entirely new additional entity might require a restructuring of an existing architecture or extending it to a new version, depending in which stage the system is receiving these new requirements.

It may be very enticing to just add an additional dependency to an existing orchestration service - but that's where the system starts to diverge from 'The Standard'. And that's when the system starts off the road of being an unmaintainable legacy system. But more importantly, it's when the engineers involved in designing and developing the system are challenged against their very principles and craftmanship.

2.3.2.1.1.2 No-Normalization

There are scenarios where any level of normalization is a challenge to achieve. While I believe that everything, everywhere, somehow is connected. Sometimes it might be incomprehensible for the mind to group multiple services together under one orchestration service.

Because it's quite hard for my mind to come up with an example for multiple entities that have no connection to each other, as I truly believe it couldn't exist. I'm going to rely on some fictional entities to visualize a problem. So let's assume there are `AService` and `BService` orchestrated together with an `XService`. The existence of `XService` is important to ensure that both `A` and `B` can be created with an assurance that a core entity `X` does exist.

Now, let's say a new service `CService` is required to be added to the mix to complete the existing flow. So, now we have four different dependencies under one orchestration service, and a split is mandatory. Since there's no relationship whatsoever between A, B and C, a 'No-Normalization' approach becomes the only option to realize a new design as follows:

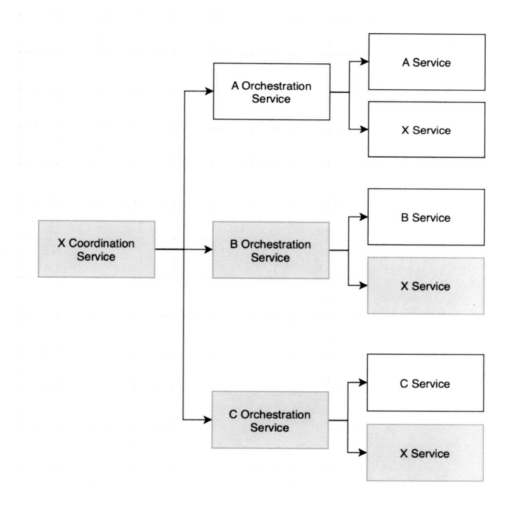

Each one of the above primitive services will be orchestrated with a core service X then gathered again under a coordination service. This case above is the worst case scenario, where a normalization of any size is impossible. Note, that the author of this Standard couldn't come up with a realistic example unlike any others to show you how rare it is to run into that situation, so let's a 'No-Normalization' approach be your very last solution if you truly run out of options.

2.3.2.1.1.3 Meaningful Breakdown

Regardless of the type of normalization that you will need to follow. You have to make sure that your grouped services represent a common meaning. For instance, putting together a `StudentProcessingService` and `LibraryPro cessingService` must require a commonality in function between the two. A good example of that would be `StudentRegistrationOrchestrationServ ice` for instance. The registration process requires adding a new student record and creating a library card for that very same student.

Implementing orchestration services without intersection between two or three entities per operation defeats the whole purpose of having an orchestration service. This condition is satisfied if at least one intersection between two entities has occurred. An orchestration service may then have other operations that we call 'Pass-Through' where we propagate certain routines from their processing or foundation origins if they match the same contract.

Here's an example:

```
public class StudentOrchestrationService
{
    public async ValueTask<Student> RegisterStudentAsync(Student student)
    {
        Student addedStudent =
            await this.studentProcessingService.AddStudentAsync(student);

        LibraryCard libraryCard =
            await this.libraryCardPorcessingService.AddLibraryCardAsync(
                addedStudent.Id);

        return addedStudent;
    }

    public async ValueTask<Student> ModifyStudentAsync(Student student) =>
        await this.studentProcessingService.ModifyStudentAsync(student);
}
```

In the example above, our `StudentOrchestrationService` had an orchestration routine where it combined adding a student and creating a library card for that very same student. But additionally it also offers a 'Pass-Through' function for a low-level processing service routine to modify a student.

'Pass-Through' routines must have the exact same contract as the rest of all other routines in any orchestration service. That's our 'Pure Contract' principle which dictates that any service should allow the very same contract as input and output or primitive types.

2.3.2.2 Contracts

Orchestration services may combine two or three different entities and their operations to achieve an advanced business logic. There are two situations when it comes to contract/models for orchestration services. One that stays true to the main entity of purpose. And one that is complex - a combinator orchestration service that tries to explicitly expose it's inner target entities.

Let's talk about these two scenarios in detail.

2.3.2.2.0 Physical Contracts

Some orchestration services are still single-purposed even though they may be combining two or three other higher order routines from multiple entities. For instance, an orchestration service that reacts to messages from some queue then persists these messages are single-purposed and single-entity orchestration services.

Let's take a look at this code snippet:

```
public class StudentOrchestrationService
{
    private readonly IStudentEventProcessingService studentEventProcessingService;
    private readonly IStudentProcessingService studentProcessingService;

    public StudentOrchestrationService(
        IStudentEventProcessingService studentEventProcessingService,
        IStudentProcessingService studentProcessingService)
    {
        this.studentEventProcessingService = studentEventProcessingService;
        this.studentProcessingService = studentProcessingService;
        ListenToEvents();
    }

    public void ListenToEvents() =>
        this.studentEventService.ListenToEvent(UpsertStudentAsync);

    public async ValueTask<Student> UpsertStudentAsync(Student student)
    {
        ...
        await this.studentProcessingService.UpsertStudentAsync(student);

        ...
    }
}
```

In the above example, the orchestration service still exposes a functionality that honors the physical model Student and internally communicates with several services that may provide completely different models. These are the scenarios where there's a main purpose single entity and all other services are supporting services to ensure a successful flow for that very entity succeeds.

In our example here, the orchestration services *listens* to a queue where new student messages will be placed, then use that event to persist any incoming new students in the system. So the physical contract Student is the same language the orchestration service explicitly use as a model to communicate with upper stream services/exposers or others.

But there are other scenarios where a single entity is not the only purpose/target for an orchestration service. Let's talk about that in detail.

2.3.2.2.1 Virtual Contracts

In some scenarios, an orchestration service may be required to create it's own non-physical contracts to complete a certain operation. For instance, consider an orchestration service that is required to persist a social media post with a picture attached to it. The requirement here is to persist the picture in one database table, and the actual post (comments, authors and others) into a different database table in a relational model.

Now, the incoming model might be significantly different from what the actual physical models would look like. Let's take a look at how would that look like in the real-world.

Consider having this model:

```
public class MediaPost
{
    public Guid Id {get; set;}
    public string Content {get; set;}
    public DateTimeOffset Date {get; set;}
    public IEnumerable<string> Base64Images {get; set;}
}
```

The above contract MediaPost contains two different physical entities combined. The first is the actual post, including the Id, Content and Date and the second is the list of images attached to that very post.

here's how an orchestration service would react to this incoming virtual model:

```csharp
public async ValueTask<MediaPost> SubmitMediaPostAsync(MediaPost mediaPost)
{
    ...

    Post post = MapToPost(mediaPost);
    List<Media> medias = MapToMedias(mediaPost);

    Post addedPost =
        await this.postProcessingService.AddPostAsync(post);

    List<Medias> addedMedias =
        await this.mediaProcessingService.AddMediasAsync(medias);

    return MapToMediaPost(addedPost, addedMedias);
}
public Post MapToPost(MediaPost mediaPost)
{
    return new Post
    {
        Id = mediaPost.Id,
        Content = mediaPost.Content,
        CreatedDate = mediaPost.Date,
        UpdatedDate = mediaPost.Date
    };
}
public List<Media> MapToMedias(MediaPost mediaPost)
{
    return mediaPost.Base64Images.Select(image =>
        new Media
        {
            Id = Guid.NewGuid(),
            PostId = mediaPost.Id,
            Image = image,
            CreatedDate = mediaPost.Date,
            UpdatedDate = mediaPost.Date
        });
}
```

The above code snippet shows the orchestration service deconstructing a
given virtual model/contract MediaPost into two physical models, each one
of them has it's own separate processing service that handles it's persistence.
There are scenarios also where the virtual model gets deconstructed into one
single model with additional details that are used for validation and
verification with downstream processing or foundation services.

There are also hybrid situations where the incoming virtual model may have
nested physical models in it. Which is something we can only allow with
virtual models. Physical models shall stay anemic (contains no routines or
constructors) and flat (contains no nested models) at all times to control
complexity and focus responsibility.

In summary, Orchestration services may create their own contracts. These
contracts may be physical or virtual. And a virtual contract may be a
combination of one or many physical (or nested virtual) contracts or simply
has it's own flat design in terms of properties.

2.3.2.2 Cul-De-Sac

There are times where Orchestration services and it's equivalent (coordination, management ... etc.) may not need an exposer component (controller for instance). That's because these services may be listeners to certain events and communicating the event back into a processing or a foundation service at the same level where the event started or was received.

For instance, imagine building a simple application where it gets notified with messages from a queue then maps these messages into some local model to persist it in storage. In this case here, the incoming or input for these services isn't necessarily through an exposer component anymore. The incoming messages can be received from a subscription to an event service or a queue. In this case the orchestration service would look something like the following:

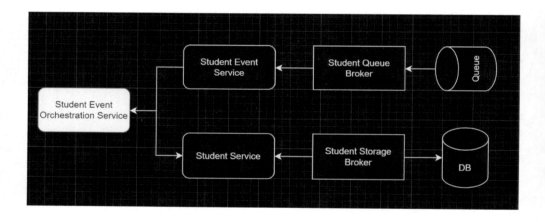

The `StudentEventOrchestrationService` in this case, listens to the messages for new students coming in and immediately converts that into models that can be persisted in the database.

Here's an example:

Let's start with a unit test for this pattern as follows:

```
[Fact]
public void ShouldListenToProfileEvents()
{
    // given . when
    this.profileEventOrchestrationService.ListenToProfileEvents();

    // then
    this.profileEventServiceMock.Verify(service =>
        service.ListenToProfileEvent(
            this.profileEventOrchestrationService.ProcessProfileEventAsync),
            Times.Once);

    this.profileEventService.VerifyNoOtherCalls();
    this.profileServiceMock.VerifyNoOtherCalls();
    this.loggingBrokerMock.VerifyNoOtherCalls();
}

[Fact]
public async Task ShouldAddProfileAsync()
{
    // given
    ProfileEvent randomProfileEvent =
        CreateRandomProfileEvent();

    ProfileEvent inputProfileEvent =
        randomProfileEvent;

    this.profileServiceMock.Setup(service =>
        service.AddProfileAsync(inputProfileEvent.Profile));

    // when
    await this.profileEventOrchestrationService
        .ProcessProfileEventAsync(inputProfileEvent);

    // then
    this.profileServiceMock.Verify(service =>
        service.AddProfileAsync(inputProfileEvent.Profile),
            Times.Once);

    this.profileServiceMock.VerifyNoOtherCalls();
    this.loggingBrokerMock.VerifyNoOtherCalls();
    this.profileEventServiceMock.VerifyNoOtherCalls();
}
```

The test here indicates an event listening has to occur first, then a persistence
in the student service must match the outcome of mapping an incoming
message to a given student.

Let's try to make this test pass.

```
public partial class ProfileEventOrchestrationService : IProfileEventOrchestrationService
{
    private readonly IProfileEventService profileEventService;
    private readonly IProfileService profileService;
    private readonly ILoggingBroker loggingBroker;

    public ProfileEventOrchestrationService(
        IProfileEventProcessingService profileEventService,
        IProfileProcessingService profileService,
        ILoggingBroker loggingBroker)
    {
        this.profileEventService = profileEventService;
        this.profileService = profileService;
        this.loggingBroker = loggingBroker;
    }

    public void ListenToProfileEvents() =>
    TryCatch(() =>
    {
        this.profileEventService.ListenToProfileEvent(
            ProcessProfileEventAsync);
    });

    public ValueTask ProcessProfileEventAsync(ProfileEvent profileEvent) =>
    TryCatch(async () =>
    {
        ...

        await this.profileService.AddProfileAsync(profileEvent.Profile);
    });
}
```

In the above example, the constructor of the Orchestration service subscribes to the events that would come from the `StudentEventService`, when an event occurs, the orchestration service will call the `ProcessingIncomingSt udentMessageAsync` function to persist the incoming student into the database through a foundation or a processing service at the same level as the event service.

This pattern or characteristic is called the Cul-De-Sac. Where an incoming message will be a turn and head in a different direction for a different dependency. This pattern is very common is large enterprise-level applications where eventual-consistency is incorporated to ensure the system can scale and become resilient under heavy consumption. This pattern also prevents malicious attacks against your API endpoints since it allows processing queue messages or events whenever the service is ready to process them. We will discuss the details in the 'The Standard Architecture'.

2.3.3 Responsibilities

Orchestration services provide an advanced business logic. It orchestrates multiple flows for multiple entities/models to complete a single flow. Let's discuss in detail what these responsibilities are:

2.3.3.0 Advanced Logic

Orchestration services cannot exist without combining multiple routines from multiple entities. These entities may be different in nature, but they share a common flow or purpose. For instance, a `LibraryCard` as a model is fundamentally different from a `Student` model. However, they both share common purpose when it comes to student registration process. Adding a student record is required to register a student, but also assigning a library card to that very same student is a requirement for a successful student registration process.

Orchestration services ensures the correct routines for each entity are integrated, but also ensures these routines are called in the right order. Additionally, orchestration services are responsible for rolling back in case of a failing operation if needed. These three aspects are what constitutes an orchestration effort across multiple routines, entities or contracts.

Let's talk about those in detail.

2.3.3.0.0 Flow Combinations

We spoke earlier about orchestration services combining multiple routines to achieve a common purpose or a single flow. This aspect of orchestration services can serve as both a fundamental characteristic but also a responsibility. And orchestration service without at least one routine that combines two or three entities is not considered truly an orchestration. Integrating with multiple services without a common purpose is a better fit definition for Aggregation services which we will discuss later in this services chapter.

But within the flow combination comes the unification of contract. I call it mapping and branching. Mapping an incoming model into multiple lower-stream services models then branching the responsibility across these services.

Just like the previous services, Orchestration services are responsible during their flow combination to ensure the purity of the exposed input and output contracts. Which becomes a bit more complex when combining multiple models. Orchestration services will continue to be responsible for mapping incoming contracts to their respective downstream services, but also ensures to map back the returned results from these services into the unified model.

Let's bring back a previous code snippet to illustrate that aspect:

```
public async ValueTask<MediaPost> SubmitMediaPostAsync(MediaPost mediaPost)
{
    ...

    Post post = MapToPost(mediaPost);
    List<Media> medias = MapToMedias(mediaPost);

    Post addedPost =
        await this.postProcessingService.AddPostAsync(post);

    List<Medias> addedMedias =
        await this.mediaProcessingService.AddMediasAsync(medias);

    return MapToMediaPost(addedPost, addedMedias);
}

private Post MapToPost(MediaPost mediaPost)
{
    return new Post
    {
        Id = mediaPost.Id,
        Content = mediaPost.Content,
        CreatedDate = mediaPost.Date,
        UpdatedDate = mediaPost.Date
    };
}

private List<Media> MapToMedias(MediaPost mediaPost)
{
    return mediaPost.Base64Images.Select(image =>
        new Media
        {
            Id = Guid.NewGuid(),
            PostId = mediaPost.Id,
            Image = image,
            CreatedDate = mediaPost.Date,
            UpdatedDate = mediaPost.Date
        });
}

private MediaPost MapToMediaPost(Post post, List<Media> medias)
{
    return new MediaPost
    {
        Id = post.Id,
        Content = post.Content,
        Date = post.CreatedDate,
        Base64Images = medias.Select(media => media.Image)
    }
}
```

As you can see in the above example, the mapping and branching doesn't just happen on the way in. But a reverse action has to be taken on the way out. It's a violation of The Standard to return the same input object that was passed in. That takes away any visibility on any potential changes that happened to the incoming request during persistence. The duplex mapping should substitute the need to dereference the incoming request to ensure no unexpected internal changes have occurred.

Note that it's also recommended to break the mapping logic into its own aspect/partial class file. Something like `StudentOrchestrationService.Mappings.cs` to make sure the only thing left there is the business logic of orchestration.

2.3.3.0.1 Call Order

Calling routines in the right order can be crucial to any orchestration process. For instance, a library card cannot be created unless a student record is created first. Enforcing the order here can split into two different types. Let's talk about those here for a bit.

2.3.3.0.1.0 Natural Order

The natural order here refers to certain flows that cannot be executed unless a prerequisite of input parameters is retrieved or persisted. For instance, imagine a situation where a library card cannot be created unless a student unique identifier is retrieved first. In this case here we don't have to worry about testing certain routines were called in the right order because it comes naturally with the flow.

here's a code example of this situation:

```
public async ValueTask<LibraryCard> CreateLibraryCardAsync(LibraryCard libraryCard)
{
    Student student = await this.studentProcessingService
        .RetrieveStudentByIdAsync(libraryCard.StudentId));

    return await this.libraryCardProcessingService
        .CreateLibraryCardAsync(libraryCard, student.Name);
}
```

In the example above, having a student `Name` is a requirement to create a library card. Therefore, the orchestration of order here comes naturally as part of the flow without any additional effort.

Let's talk about the second type of order - Enforced Order.

2.3.3.0.1.1 Enforced Order

Imagine the very same example above, but instead of the library card requiring a student name it instead just needs the student `Id` which is already enclosed in the incoming request model. Something like this:

```
public async ValueTask<LibraryCard> CreateLibraryCardAsync(LibraryCard libraryCard)
{
    await this.studentProcessingService.VerifyEnlistedStudentExistAsync(
        libraryCard.StudentId);

    return await this.libraryCardProcessingService.CreateLibraryCardAsync(libraryCard);
}
```

ensuring a verify enlisted student exists has happened before creating a library card might become a challenge to achieve naturally because there's no dependency between a return value of one routine and the input parameters of the next. In other words, there is nothing that the `VerifyEnl istedStudentExistAsync` function returns that the `CreateLibraryCardA sync` function cares about in terms of input parameters.

In this case here an enforced type of order must be implemented through unit tests. A unit test for this routine would require to verify not just the dependency have been called with the right parameters, but also that they are called in the right *order* let's take a look at how that would be implemented:

```
[Fact]
public async Task ShouldCreateLibraryCardAsync()
{
    // given
    Student someStudent = CreateRandomStudent();
    LibraryCard randomLibraryCard = CreateRandomLibraryCard();
    LibraryCard inputLibraryCard = randomLibraryCard;
    LibraryCard createdLibraryCard = inputLibraryCard;
    LibraryCard expectedLibraryCard = inputLibraryCard.DeepClone();
    Guid studentId = inputLibraryCard.StudentId;
    var mockSequence = new MockSequence();

    this.studentProcessingServiceMock.InSequence(mockSequence).Setup(service =>
        service.VerifyEnlistedStudentExistAsync(studentId))
            .Returns(someStudent);

    this.libraryCardProcessingServiceMock.InSequence(mockSequence).Setup(service =>
        service.CreateLibraryCardAsync(inputLibraryCard))
            .ReturnsAsync(createdLibraryCard);

    // when
    LibraryCard actualLibraryCard = await this.libraryCardOrchestrationService
        .CreateLibraryCardAsync(inputLibraryCard);

    // then
    actualLibraryCard.Should().BeEquivalentTo(expectedLibraryCard);

    this.studentProcessingServiceMock.Verify(service =>
        service.VerifyEnlistedStudentExistAsync(studentId),
            Times.Once);

    this.libraryCardProcessingServiceMock.Verify(service =>
        service.CreateLibraryCardAsync(inputLibraryCard),
            Times.Once);

    this.studentProcessingServiceMock.VerifyNoOtherCalls();
    this.libraryCardProcessingServiceMock.VerifyNoOtherCalls();
    this.loggingBrokerMock.VerifyNoOtherCalls();
}
```

From the example above, the mock framework here is being used to ensure a
certain order is being enforced when it comes to calling these dependencies.
This way we enforce a certain implementation within any given method to
ensure a non-naturally connected dependencies are being sequentially called
in the exact right order.

It's more likely that the form of ordering leans more towards enforced than
natural when orchestration services reach the maximum number of
dependencies they may have at any point in time.

2.3.3.0.2 Exceptions Mapping (Wrapping & Unwrapping)

This responsibility is very similar to flow-combinations. Except that in this
case orchestration services unify all the exceptions that may occur out of any
of its dependencies into one unified categorical exception model. Let's start
with an illustration of what that mapping may look like:

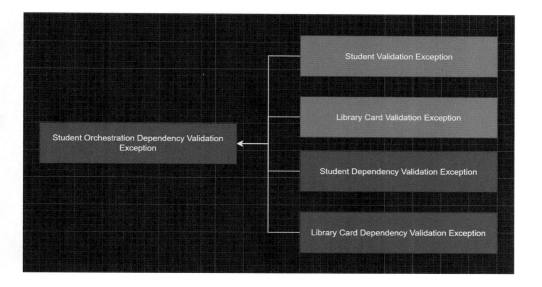

In the illustration above, you will notice that validation and dependency validation exceptions thrown from downstream dependency services are being mapped into one unified dependency exception at the orchestration level. This practice allows upstream consumers of that very orchestration service to determine the next course of action based on one categorical exception type instead of four or in the case of three dependencies it would be six categorical dependencies.

Let's start with a failing test to materialize our idea here:

```csharp
public static TheoryData DependencyValidationExceptions()
{
    string exceptionMessage = GetRandomMessage();
    var innerException = new Xeption(exceptionMessage);

    var studentValidationException =
        new StudentValidationException(innerException);

    var studentDependencyValidationException =
        new StudentDependencyValidationException(innerException);

    var libraryCardValidationException =
        new LibraryCardValidationException(innerException);

    var libraryCardDependencyValidationException =
        new LibraryCardDependencyValidationException(innerException);

    return new TheoryData<Xeption>
    {
        studentValidationException,
        studentDependencyValidationException,
        libraryCardValidationException,
        libraryCardDependencyValidationException
    };
}


[Theory]
[MemberData(nameof(DependencyValidationExceptions))]
public async Task ShouldThrowDependencyValidationExceptionOnCreateIfDependencyValidationErrorOccursAndLogItAsync(
    Xeption dependencyValidationException)
{
    // given
    Student someStudent = CreateRandomStudent();

    var expectedStudentOrchestrationDependencyValidationException =
        new StudentOrchestrationDependencyValidationException(
            dependencyValidationException.InnerException as Xeption);

    this.studentServiceMock.Setup(service =>
        service.AddStudentAsync(It.IsAny<Student>()))
            .ThrowsAsync(dependencyValidationException);

    // when
    ValueTask<Student> addStudentTask =
        await this.studentOrchestrationService.AddStudentAsync(someStudent);

    StudentOrchestrationDependencyValidationException
        actualStudentOrchestrationDependencyValidationException =
            await Assert.ThrowsAsync<StudentOrchestrationDependencyValidationException>(
                addStudentTask.AsTask);

    // then
    actualStudentOrchestrationDependencyValidationException.Should()
        .BeEquivalentTo(expectedStudentOrchestrationDependencyValidationException);

    this.studentServiceMock.Verify(service =>
        service.AddStudentAsync(It.IsAny<Student>()),
            Times.Once);

    this.loggingBrokerMock.Verify(broker =>
        broker.LogError(It.Is(SameExceptionAs(
            expectedStudentOrchestrationDependencyValidationException))),
                Times.Once);

    this.libraryCardServiceMock.Verify(service =>
        service.AddLibraryCard(It.IsAny<Guid>()),
            Times.Once);

    this.studentServiceMock.VerifyNoOtherCalls();
    this.loggingBrokerMock.VerifyNoOtherCalls();
    this.libraryCardServiceMock.VerifyNoOtherCalls();
}
```

In the test above, we are verifying that any of the four aforementioned
exceptions on occurrence, they would be mapped into a `StudentOrchestra
tionDependencyValidationException`. We maintain the original localized
exception as an inner exception. But we unwrap the categorical exception at
this level to maintain the original issue as we go upstream.

These exceptions are mapped under a dependency validation exception because they originate from a dependency or a dependency of a dependency downstream. For instance, if a storage broker throws an exception that is deemed to be a dependency validation (something like `DuplicateKeyException`). The broker-neighboring service would map that into a localized `StudentAlredyExistException` then wrap that exception in a categorical exception of type `StudentDependencyValidationException`. When that exception propagates upstream to a processing or an orchestration service, we lose the categorical exception as we have already captured it under the right scope of mapping. Then we continue to embed that very localized exception under the current service dependency validation exception.

Let's try to make this test pass:

```
public partial class StudentOrchestrationService
{
    private delegate ValueTask<Student> ReturningStudentFunction();

    private async ValueTask<Student> TryCatch(ReturningStudentFunction returningStudentFunction)
    {
        try
        {
            return await returningStudentFunction();
        }
        catch (StudentValidationException studentValidationException)
        {
            throw CreateAndLogDependencyValidationException(studentValidationException);
        }
        catch (StudentDependencyValidationException studentDependencyValidationException)
        {
            throw CreateAndLogDependencyValidationException(studentDependencyValidationException);
        }
        catch (LibraryCardValidationException libraryCardValidationException)
        {
            throw CreateAndLogDependencyValidationException(libraryCardValidationException);
        }
        catch (LibraryCardDependencyValidationException libraryCardDependencyValidationException)
        {
            throw CreateAndLogDependencyValidationException(libraryCardDependencyValidationException);
        }
    }

    private StudentOrchestrationDependencyValidationException CreateAndLogDependencyValidationException(Xeption exception)
    {
        var studentOrchestrationDependencyValidationException =
            new StudentOrchestrationDependencyValidationException(exception.innerException as Xeption);

        this.loggingBroker.LogError(studentOrchestrationDependencyValidationException);

        throw studentOrchestrationDependencyValidationException;
    }
}
```

Now we can use the `TryCatch` as follows:

```
public async ValueTask<Student> AddStudentAsync(Student student) =>
TryCatch(async () =>
{
    ...
    Student addedStudent = await this.studentService.AddStudentAsync(student);
    LibraryCard libraryCard = await this.libraryCard.AddLibraryCard(addedStudent.Id);

    return addedStudent;
});
```

You can see now in the implementation that we mapped all four different types of external downstream services validation exceptions into one categorical exception and then maintained the inner exception for each one of them.

The same rule applies to dependency exceptions. Dependency exceptions can be both Service and Dependency exceptions from downstream services. For instance, in the above example, calling a student service may produce `Stude ntDependencyException` and `StudentServiceException`. Both of these categorical exceptions will be unwrapped from their categorical layer and have their local layer wrapped in one unified new orchestration-level categorical exception under `StudentOrchestrationDependencyException`. The same thing applies to all other dependency categorical exceptions like `LibraryCardDependencyE xception` and `LibraryCardServiceException`.

It's extremely important to unwrap and wrap localized exceptions from downstream services with categorical exceptions at the current service layer to ensure at the Exposers layer these exceptions can be easily handled and mapped into whatever the nature of the exposer component dictates. In the case of an Exposer component of type API Controller, the mapping would produce Http Status Codes. In the case of UI Exposer components it would be mapped to meaningful text to the end users.

We will discuss further upstream in this Standard when to determine to expose localized inner exceptions details where end-users are not required to take any action. This is exclusive to dependency and service level exceptions.

2.3.4 Variations

Orchestration services have several variations depending on where they stand in the overall low-level architecture. For instance, an orchestration service depending on downstream orchestration services is called a Coordination Service. An orchestration service working with multiple coordination services as dependencies is called a Management Service. These variants are all in essence an orchestration service with an uber-level business logic.

2.3.4.0 Variants Levels

Let's take a look at the possible variants for orchestration services and where they would be positioned:

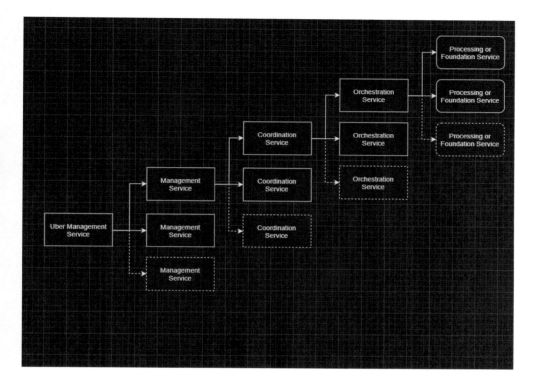

In my personal experience, I've rarely had to resolve to an Uber Management service. The idea of the limitation here in terms of dependencies and variations of orchestration-like services is to help engineers re-think the complexity of their logic. But admittedly there are situations where the complexity is an absolute necessity, therefore Uber-Management services exist as an option.

The following table should guide the process of developing variants of orchestration services based on the level:

Variant	Dependencies	Consumers	Complexity
Orchestrations Services	Foundation or Processing Services	Coordination Services	Low
Coordination Services	Orchestration Services	Management Services	Medium
Management Services	Coordination Services	Uber Management Services	High
Uber Management Services	Management Services	Aggregation, Views or Exposer Components	Very High

Working beyond Uber Management services in an orchestration manner would require a deeper discussion and a serious consideration of the overall architecture. Some future versions The Standard might be able to address this issue in what I call "The Lake House" but that is outside of the scope of this version of The Standard.

2.3.4.1 Unit of Work

With the variations of orchestration services, I highly recommend staying true to the unit of work concept. Where every request can do one thing and one thing only including it's pre-requisites. For instance, if you need to register a student in some school, You may require also adding a guardian, contact information and some other details. Eventing these actions can greatly decrease the complexity of the flow and lower the risk of any failures in downstream services.

Here's a visualization for a complex single-threaded approach:

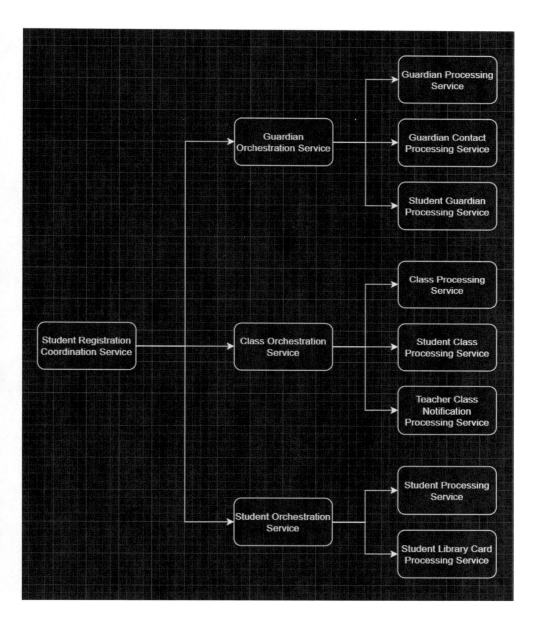

The solution above is a working solution for registering a student. We needed to include guardian information, library cards, classes ... etc. These dependencies can be broken down in terms of eventing and allowing other services to pick up where the single-threaded services leaves off to continue the registration process. Something like this:

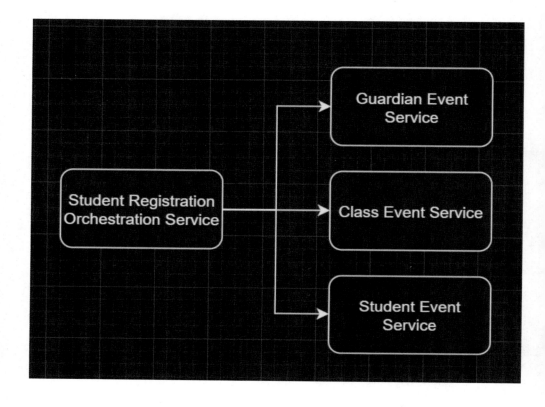

The incoming request in the above example would be turned into events, where each one of these events would be notifying its own orchestration services in a cul-de-sac manner as we discussed above in section 2.3.2.2. What that means is that a single thread is no longer responsible for the success of each and every dependency in the system. Instead, every event-listening broker would handle its own process in a much, much simplified way.

That approach does not guarantee an immediate response of success or failure to the requestor. It's an eventual-consistency pattern where the client would get an `Accepted` message or its equivalent based on the communication protocol to let them know that a process has started but there's no guarantee of any results yet until it's done.

It's also important to mention that an extra layer of resiliency can be added to these events by temporarily storing them in Queue-like components or memory-based temporary storages; depending on the criticality of the business.

But an eventual consistency approach isn't always a good solution if the client on the other side is waiting for a response. Especially in a much critical situations where an immediate response is required. This problem can be solved through Fire-n-Observe queues that we will discuss in future version of The Standard.

[*] Introduction to Orchestration Services

[*] Cul-De-Sac Pattern for Orchestration Services

[*] Cul-De-Sac Pattern for Coordination Services

2.4 Aggregation Services (The Knot)

2.4.0 Introduction

Aggregation services main responsibility is to expose one single point of contact between the core business logic layer and any exposure layers. It ensures, if multiple services of any variation share the same contract, that they are aggregated and exposed to one exposer component through one logical layer.

Aggregation services don't hold any business logic in themselves. They are simply a knot that ties together multiple services of any number. They can have any layer of services as dependencies and it mainly exposes the call to these services accordingly. Here's a code example of an aggregation service:

```
public async ValueTask ProcessStudentAsync(Student student)
{
    await this.studentRegistrationCoordinationService.RegisterStudentAsync(student);
    await this.studentRecordsCoordinationService.AddStudentRecordAsync(student);
    ...
    ...
    await this.anyOtherStudentRelatedCoordinationService.DoSomethingWithStudentAsync(student);
}
```

As the snippet shows above, an Aggregation service may have any number of calls in any order without limitation. And there may be occasions where you may or may not need to return a value to your exposure layers depending on the overall flow and architecture, which we will discuss shortly in this chapter. But more importantly Aggregation services should not be mistaken for an orchestration service or any of its variants.

2.4.1 On The Map

Aggregation services always sit on the other end of a core business logic layer. They are the last point of contact between exposure layers and logic layers. here's a visualization of where aggregation services would be located in an overall architecture:

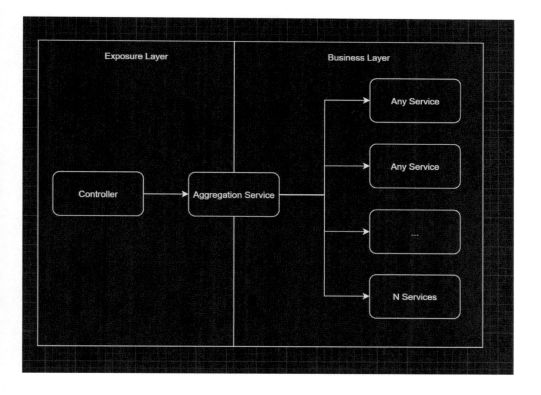

Let's discuss the characteristics of Aggregation services.

2.4.2 Characteristics

Aggregation services mainly exist when there are multiple services, sharing the same contract or sharing primitive types of the same contract, that require a single point of exposure. They mainly exist in hyper-complex applications where multiple services (usually orchestration or higher but can be lower) require one single point of contact through exposure layers. Let's talk in detail about the main characteristics for Aggregation services.

2.4.2.0 No Dependency Limitation

Unlike any other service, Aggregation services can have any number of dependencies as long as these services are of the same variation. For instance, an Aggregation service cannot aggregate between an Orchestration service and a Coordination service. It's a partial Florance-Like pattern where services have to be of the same variation but not necessary limited by the number.

The reason for the lack of limitation of the dependencies for Aggregation services is because the service itself doesn't perform any level of business logic between these services. It doesn't care what these services do or require. It only focuses on exposing these services regardless of what was called before or after them.

Here's what an Aggregation service test would look like:

```
[Fact]
public async Task ShouldProcessStudentAsync()
{
    // given
    Student randomStudent = CreatedRandomStudent();
    Student inputStudent = randomStudent;

    // when
    await this.studentAggregationService.ProcessStudentAsync(inputStudent);

    // then
    this.studentRegistrationCoordinationServiceMock.Verify(service =>
        service.RegisterStudentAsync(student),
            Times.Once);

    this.studentRecordsCoordinationServiceMock.Verify(service =>
        service.AddStudentRecordAsync(student),
            Times.Once);
    ...
    ...

    this.anyOtherStudentRelatedCoordinationServiceMock.Verify(service =>
        service.DoSomethingWithStudentAsync(student),
            Times.Once);

    this.studentRegistrationCoordinationServiceMock.VerifyNoOtherCalls();
    this.studentRecordsCoordinationServiceMock.VerifyNoOtherCalls();
    ...
    ...
    this.anyOtherStudentRelatedCoordinationServiceMock.VerifyNoOtherCalls();
}
```

As you can see above, we are only verifying and testing for the aggregation aspect of calling these services. No return type required in this scenario but there might be in the scenarios of pass-through which we will be discussing shortly.

An implementation of the above test would be as follows:

```
public async ValueTask ProcessStudentAsync(Student student)
{
    await this.studentRegistrationCoordinationService.RegisterStudentAsync(student);
    await this.studentRecordsCoordinationService.AddStudentRecordAsync(student);
    ...
    ...
    await this.anyOtherStudentRelatedCoordinationService.DoSomethingWithStudentAsync(student);
}
```

2.4.2.1 No Order Validation

By definition, Aggregation services are naturally required to call several dependencies with no limitation. The order of calling these dependencies is also not a concern or a responsibility for Aggregation services. That's simply because the call-order verification is considered a core business logic. which falls outside of the responsibilities of an Aggregation service. That of course includes both natural order of verification or enforced order of verification as we explained in section 2.3.3.0.1 in the previous chapter.

It's a violation of The Standard to attempt using simple techniques like a mock sequence in testing an Aggregation service. These responsibilities are more likely to fall on the next lower layer of an Aggregation service for any orchestration-like service. It is also a violation to verify reliance on the return value of one service call to initiate a call to the next.

2.4.2.2 Basic Validations

Aggregation services are still required to validate whether the incoming data is higher-level structurally valid or not. For instance, an Aggregation service that takes a `Student` object as an input parameter will validate only if the `student` is `null` or not. But that's where it all stops.

There may be an occasion where a dependency requires a property of an input parameter to be passed in, in which case it is also permitted to validate that property value structurally. For instance, if a downstream dependency requires a student name to be passed in. An Aggregation service is still going to be required to validate if the `Name` is `null`, empty or just whitespace.

2.4.2.3 Pass-Through

Aggregation services are not also required to implement their aggregation by performing multiple calls from one method. They can also aggregate by offering a pass-through methods for multiple services. For instance, assume we have `studentCoordinationService` and `studentRecordsService` and `anyOtherStudentRelatedCoordinationService` and each one of these services are independent in terms of business flow. So an aggregation here is only at the level of exposure but not necessarily the level of execution.

Here's a code example:

```csharp
public partial class StudentAggregationService
{
    ...

    public async ValueTask<Student> RegisterStudentAsync(Student student)
    {
        ...

        return await this.studentCoordinationService.RegisterStudentAsync(student);
    }
    public async ValueTask<Student> AddStudentRecordAsync(Student student)
    {
        ...

        return await this.studentRecordsCoordinationService.AddStudentRecordAsync(student);
    }

    ...
    ...

    public async ValueTask<Student> DoSomethingWithStudentAsync(Student student)
    {
        ...

        return await this.anyOtherStudentRelatedCoordinationService.DoSomethingWithStudentAsync(student);
    }
}
```

As you can see above, each service is using the Aggregation service as a pass-through. There's no need in this scenario whatsoever for an aggregated routines call. This would still be a very valid scenario for Aggregation services.

2.4.2.4 Optionality

It is important to mention here that Aggregation services are optional. Unlike foundation services, Aggregation services may or may not exist in any architecture. Aggregation services are there to solve a problem with abstraction. This problem may or may not exist based on whether the architecture requires a single point of exposure at the border of the core business logic layer or not. This single responsibility of Aggregation services makes it much simpler to implement its task and perform its function easily. Aggregation services being optional is more likely to be than any other lower-level services. Even in the most complex of applications out there.

2.4.2.5 Routine-Level Aggregation

If an aggregation service has to make two different calls from the same dependency amongst other calls, It is recommended to aggregate for every dependency routine. But that's only from code-cleanliness perspective and it doesn't necessarily impact the architecture or the end-result in any way.

here's an example:

```
public async ValueTask ProcessStudent(Student student)
{
    await this.studentCoordinationService.AddStudentAsync(student);
    await ProcessStudentRecordAsync(student);
}

private async ValueTask ProcessStudentRecordAsync(Student student)
{
    await this.studentRecordCoordinationService.AddStudentRecordAsync(student);
    await this.studentRecordCoordinationService.NotifyStudentRecordAdminsAsync(student);
}
```

This organizational action doesn't warrant any kind of change in terms of testing or end-result as previously mentioned.

2.4.2.6 Pure Dependency Contracts

The most important rule/characteristic of an Aggregation service is that its dependencies (unlike orchestration services) must share the same contract. The input parameter for a public routine in any Aggregation service must be the same for all its dependencies. There may be occasions where a dependency may require a student id instead of of the entire student that is permitted with caution as long as the partial contract isn't a return type of another call within the same routine.

2.4.3 Responsibilities

Aggregation services main responsibility is to offer a single point of contact between exposer components and the rest of the core business logic. But in essence, abstraction is the true value Aggregation services offer to ensure any business component as a whole is pluggable into any system regardless of the style of exposure this very system may need.

Let's talk about these responsibilities in detail.

2.4.3.0 Abstraction

An aggregation service performs into responsibility successfully when its clients or consumers have no idea what lies beyond the lines of its implementation. An Aggregation service could be combining 10 different services and exposes a single routine in a fire-n-forget scenario.

But even in pass-through scenarios, Aggregation services abstract away any identification of the underlying dependency from exposers at all costs. It doesn't always happen especially in terms of localized exceptions but close enough to make the integration seem as if it is with one single service that's offering all the options natively.

2.4.3.1 Exceptions Aggregation

Aggregation services are also similar to orchestration-like services in terms of mapping and aggregating exceptions from downstream dependencies. For instance, if `studentCoordinationService` is throwing `StudentCoordinationValidationException` an Aggregation service would map that into `StudentAggregationDependencyValidationException`. This falls back into the concept of exception unwrapping then wrapping of localized exceptions which we spoke about in detail in section 2.3.3.0.2 of this Standard.

3 Exposers
3.0 Introduction

Exposers are disposable components in any system that has the single responsibility of exposing your core business logic functionality by mapping its responses to a certain protocol. For instance, in RESTful communications, an API controller would be responsible for returning a 200 code for a successful response. The same thing applies to other protocols such as gRPC or SOAP or any other protocol of communication between distributed systems.

Exposer components are similar to Brokers. They are the last point of contact between the core business logic and the outside world. They are built with the intent that they will be detached from the current system at some point in time to allow the very same core logic to integrate with modern systems, protocols or interfaces.

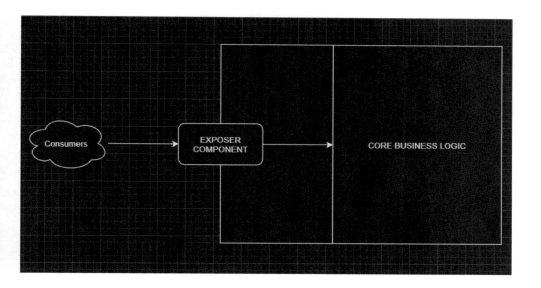

3.0.0 Purpose

In general, exposure components main responsibility is to allow someone or something to interact with your business logic. In that core purpose a precise mapping bit by bit to every possible response from your core business logic should be communicated cautiously with the consumer to that logic. I say cautiously because sometimes certain internal issues in the system are not required to be exposed to the outside world. This mapping of responses can usually be a zero effort as the protocol and the language your code business logic communicate are the same such as the case with libraries produced to run on the system that use the same technologies or programming languages.

But there are occassions where the outside world stateless protocol doesn't necessarily match the same value of a response. In which case it becomes an exposer component responsibility to make a successful mapping both ways in and out of the system. API controllers are a great example of that. They will communicate a 4xx issue when there's a validation exception of some type and return a deserialized JSON value if the communication was successful. But there are also more details around problem details, error codes and other levels of mapping and communication that we will discuss in upcoming chapters within this section.

3.0.0.0 Pure Mapping

The most important aspect of exposure components is that they are not allowed to communicate with brokers of any type. And they are not allowed to contain any form of business logic within them. By business logic here I mean no sequence of routine calls, no iteration or selection/decision making. The same way it is with brokers, they only link an existing realm with the outside realm to achieve a certain value.

3.0.1 Types of Exposure Components

Exposure components have three different types. Which are either communication protocols, user interfaces or simply an IO routine. Let's talk about those breifly.

3.0.1.0 Communication Protocols

An exposure component that is a communication protocol can vary from simple RESTful APIs, to SOAP communication or gRPC. They can also be a simple client in a library where consumers would just install the library in their projects and consume your core logic through the client APIs. These examples are all of the same type of exposure components.

The differentiator here is that a communication protocol is usually event-based. Triggered by an incoming communication and treated with a response of any kind. Communication protocols are usually for system-to-system integrations but they can be accessible and understandble by humans for testing and debugging purposes.

3.0.1.1 User Interfaces

Another type of exposer components are user interfaces. This can vary from Web, mobile or desktop applications including simple command lines. They mainly target end-users for communication but can be automated by other systems. Especially with command line user interfaces.In this day and age, user interfaces can also include virtual and augmented realities, metaverses and any other form of software.

There are occasions where Human-Machine-Interfaces (HMI) can also fall into that level of exposure components. For instance, the buttons on a cellphone, keyboards we use everyday and any form of hardware that can interact directly with core business logic interfaces as an exposure component. The same theory applies to the Internet of Things (IoT) components and many others where a human has to utilize a component to leverage a certain capability to their own advantage in anyway.

3.0.1.2 I/O Components

Some exposure components are not necessarily a system interfacing with another system. Neither they are purposed to communicate with humans. They are daemons or IO based components that do something in the background without a trigger. usually these components are time-based and they may leverage existing protocols or just simply interface directly with the core business logic which are both viable options.

3.0.2 Single Point of Contact

Exposure components are only allowed to communicate with one and only one service. Integrating with multiple services would turn an exposure component into either orchestration or aggregation services which are both not allowed to exist as core logic in that realm of exposure.

The single point of contact rule also ensures the ease of disposability of the exposure component itself. It ensures the integration is simple and single-purposed enough with controlled dependencies (only one) that it can be rewired to virtually any protocol at any point in time with the least cost possible.

3.0.3 Examples

Let's take API controllers as an example for a real-world exposure component in any given system.

```
[HttpPost]
public async ValueTask<ActionResult<Student>> PostStudentAsync(Student student)
{
    try
    {
        Student registeredStudent =
            await this.studentService.RegisterStudentAsync(student);

        return Created(registeredStudent);
    }
    catch (StudentValidationException studentValidationException)
        when (studentValidationException.InnerException is AlreadyExistsStudentException)
    {
        return Conflict(studentValidationException.InnerException);
    }
    catch (StudentValidationException studentValidationException)
    {
        return BadRequest(studentValidationException.InnerException);
    }
    catch (StudentDependencyException studentDependencyException)
    {
        return InternalServerError(studentDependencyException);
    }
    catch (StudentServiceException studentServiceException)
    {
        return InternalServerError(studentServiceException);
    }
}
```

The code snippet above is for an API method that POST a student model into the core business logic of a schooling system (OtripleS). In a technology like ASP.NET, controllers take care of handling mapping incoming JSON request into the Student model so the controller can utilize that model with an integrated system.

However, you will also see the controller code tries to map every possible categorical exception into it's respective REST protocol. This is just a simple snippet to show what an exposure component may look like. But we will talk more about the rules and conditions for controllers in the next chapter in The Standard.

3.0.4 Summary

In summary, exposure components are very thin layer that doesn't contain any intelligence or logic in it. it is not meant to orchestrate, or call multiple core business logic services. And it only focuses on the duplex mapping aspect of the communication between one system and another.

3.1 Communication Protocols
3.1.0 Introduction

In the exposure realm, one of the most common methodologies to build a communication structure between several system is to use a communication protocol. These protocols have evolved over the years from SOAP to REST to so many other communication protocols and principles that manifested their own technologies to accomplish exposing APIs to distributed systems.

In the .NET world, technology has evolved with the evolution of architecture from SOA with WCF to Microservices with REST. The evolution continues but the principles change less often. In these upcoming chapters we will be discussing the most common communication protocols with a standardized way to implementing them for an enterprise-level applications.

3.1.0.0 Principles & Rules

Communication protocols are required to accomplish two things when integrating with core business logic. Results communication and Error reporting. Let's talk about those briefly:

3.1.0.0.0 Results Communication

Any communication protocol is required to satisfy the principle of returning core business logic result. This result can be serialized into some unified language like `JSON` or simply be communicated as is. In the case of API libraries there is usually no need to serialize and deserialize data. But that comes with the limitation that only technologies that can integrate with these libraries can actually benefit from it.

Communicating results may also be encapsulated with a status of some kind. In the case of RESTful API communications a `200` code can accompany the returned serialized `JSON` result. These codes allow the consumers to understand the next course of action. Some 2xx results may require a delayed action if the response is just `Accepted` but not necessarily `Created`.

3.1.0.0.1 Error Reports

If the core business logic is expected to provide a detailed report of all the validation errors for instance that occurred in a particular request. It is the responsibility of the communication protocols to represent these error reports either in their original form as is, or serialize the report in a language that is easily deserializable and convertable back into the Exception original form on the client side.

Error reports shall also have their own codes in case they are serialized so the client knows what the next course of action is. It is highly recommend to follow a standardized way of communicating errors with documentation preferably to help guide consumers to develop the best clients for these APIs.

3.1.0.1 Common Types

Let's explore some of the most common types of communication protocols in this section.

3.1.0.1.0 REST

At the time of authoring this Standard, RESTful APIs are the most common form of communication between distributed systems. REST is a Representational state transfer protocol with certain constraints that specifically defines the form of communication, error reporting and its very stateless nature. RESTful APIs are technology agnostic. They can be implemented by any technology or a programming language but they allow these technologies to communicate with each other statelessly without any hard dependency on the server or the client choice of technology.

3.1.0.1.1 Libraries

The other most common communication protocol is APIs implemented within libraries. For instance, nuget packages are published and distributed libraries that allow developers to leverage a localized core business logic or communicate with an external resource to achieve a certain goal.

3.1.0.1.2 Other Types

There are several other types of communication protocols. Some of them are older and some others are about to present themselves in the software industry. These types are like SOAP with manifestations like WCF and gRPC, GraphQL and several other protocols.

We will be mainly focusing on RESTful APIs as a more common communication protocols with a brief touch on Libraries. And as we evolve and learn further so will our Standard which will include more and more different communication protocols and evolve in terms of patterns as well.

Let's get started with RESTful APIs as a communication protocol and dive deeper into the different aspect of that exposer component.

3.1.1 RESTful APIs
3.1.1.0 Introduction

RESTful API controllers are a liaison between the core business logic layer and the outside world. They sit on the other side of the core business realm of any application. In a way, API Controllers are just like Brokers. They ensure a successful integration between our core logic and the rest of the world.

3.1.1.1 On the Map

Controllers sit at the edge of any system. Regardless whether this system is a monolithic platform or simple microservice. API controllers today even apply to smaller lambdas or cloud functions. They play the role of a trigger to access these resources in any system through REST.

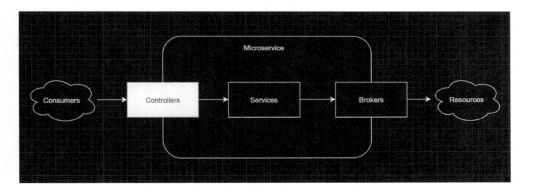

The consumer side of controllers can vary. In production systems these consumers can be other services requiring data from a particular API endpoint. They can be libraries built as wrappers around the controller APIs to provide a local resource with external data. But consumers can also be just engineers testing endpoints, validating their behaviors through swagger documents.

3.1.1.2 Characteristics

There are several rules and principles that govern the implementation of RESTful API endpoints. Let's discuss those here.

3.1.1.2.0 Language

Controllers speak a different language when it comes to implementing their methods as compared to services and brokers. For instance, if a broker that interfaces with a storage uses a language such as `InsertStudentAsync`, and its corresponding service implementation uses something like `AddStude ntAsync` the controller equivalent will be using RESTful language such as `Po stStudentAsync`.

There are only a handful of terminologies a controller would use to express a certain operation. Let's draw the map here for clarity:

Controllers	Services	Brokers
Post	Add	Insert
Get	Retrieve	Select
Put	Modify	Update
Delete	Remove	Delete

The language controllers speak is called Http Verbs. Their range are wider than the aforementioned CRUD operations. For instance, there is PATCH which allows API consumers to update only portions of a particular document. PATCH is rarely used today from my experience in productionized applications. But I may specialize a special section for them at some point in time in future versions of The Standard.

3.1.1.2.0.0 Beyond CRUD Routines

But as we mentioned before, controller can interface with more than just a foundation service. They can interface with higher-order business logic function. For instance, a processing service may offer an `Upsert` routine. In which case a typical Http Verb wouldn't be able to satisfy a combinational routine such as an `Upsert`. In which case we resolve to the intial state of `Po st` assuming the resource doesn't exist.

It may become useful to notify our consumers if we decided to modify instead of add which operation we decided to go with. But that's a case by case implementation and more often than ever, consumers don't really care to learn that piece of information. The same idea applies to other languages non-foundation services may use. Such as `Process` or `Calculate` or any other business-specific language higher or hyper advanced order services may choose.

3.1.1.2.0.1 Similar Verbs

Sometimes, especially with basic CRUD operations, you will need the same Http Verb to describe two different routines. For instnace, integrating with both `RetrieveById` and `RetrieveAll` both resolve to a `Get` operation on the RESTful realm. In which case each function will have a different name, while maintainig the same verb as follows:

```
[HttpGet]
public ActionResult<IQueryable<Student>> GetAllStudents()
{
    ...
}

[HttpGet("{studentId}")]
public async ValueTask<ActionResult<Student>> GetStudentByIdAsync(Guid studentId)
{
    ...
}
```

As you can see above, the differentiator here is both the function name `GetAllStudents` versus `GetStudentByIdAsync` but also the `Route` at the same time. We will discuss routes shortly, but the main aspect here is the ability to implement multiple routines with different names even if they resolve to the same Http Verb.

3.1.1.2.0.2 Routes Conventions

RESTful API controllers are accessible through routes. a route is simply a url that is used combined with an Http Verb so the system knows which routine it needs to call to match that route. For instance, if I need to retrieve a student with Id `123` then my api route would be as follows: `api/students/123`. And if I want to retrieve all the students in some system, I could just call `api/students` with `GET` verb.

3.1.1.2.0.2.0 Controller Routes

The controller class in a simple ASP.NET application can be simply setup at the top of the controller class declaration with a decoration as follows:

```
[ApiController]
[Route("api/[controller]")]
public class StudentsController
{
    ...
}
```

The route there is a template that defines the endpoint to start with `api` and trailed by omitting the term "Controller" from the class name. So `StudentsController` would endup being `api/students`. It's important that all controllers should have a plural version of the contract they are serving. Unlike services where we say `StudentService` controllers would be the plural version with `StudentsController`.

3.1.1.2.0.2.1 Routine Routes

The same idea applies to methods within the controller class. As we say in the code snippet above, we decorated `GetStudentByIdAsync` have had an `HttpGet` decoration with a particular route identified to append to the existing controller overall route. For instance if the controller route is `api/students`, a routine with `HttpGet("{studentId})` would result in a route that looks like this: `api/students/{studentId}`.

The `studentId` then would be mapped in as an input parameter variable that *must* match the variable defined in the route as follows:

```
[HttpGet("{studentId}")]
public async ValueTask<ActionResult<Student>> GetStudentByIdAsync(Guid studentId)
{
    ...
}
```

But sometimes these routes are not just url parameters. Sometimes they contain a request within them. For instance, let's say we want to post a library card against a particular student record. Our endpoint would look something like this: `api/students/{studentId}/librarycards` with a POST verb. In this case we have to distinguish between these two input parameters with proper naming as follows:

```
[HttpPost("{studentId}/librarycards")]
public async ValueTask<ActionResult<LibraryCard>> PostLibraryCardAsync(Guid studentId, LibraryCard libraryCard)
{
    ...
}
```

3.1.1.2.0.2.2 Plural Singular Plural

When defining routes in a RESTful API, it is important to follow the global naming conventions for these routes. The general rule is to access a collection of resources, then target a particular entity, then again acess a collection of resources within that entity and so on and so forth. For instance, in the library card example above `api/students/{studentId}/librarycards/{librarycardId}` you can see we started by accessing all students, then targetted a student with a particular id, then we wanted to access all library cards attached to that student then target a very particular card by referencing its id.

That convention works perfectly in one-to-many relationships. But what about one-to-one relationships? Let's assume a student may have one and only one library card at all times. In which case our route would still look something like this: `api/students/{studentId}/librarycards` with a POST verb, and an error would occur as `CONFLICT` if a card is already in place regardless whether the Ids match or not.

3.1.1.2.0.2.2 Query Parameters & OData

But the route I recommend is the flat-model route. Where every resource lives on it's own with it's own unique routes. In our case here pulling a library card for a particular student would be as follows: `api/librarycards?studentId={studentId}` or simply use a slightly advanced global technology such as OData where the query would just be `api/librarycards?$filter=studentId eq '123'`.

Here's an example of implementing basic query parameters:

```
[HttpPost()]
public async ValueTask<ActionResult<LibraryCard>> PostLibraryCardAsync(Guid studentId, LibraryCard libraryCard)
{
    ...
}
```

On the OData side, an implementation would be as follows:

```
[HttpGet]
[EnableQuery]
public async ValueTask<IQueryable<LibraryCard>> GetAllLibraryCards()
{
    ...
}
```

The same idea applies to `POST` for a model. instead of posting towards: `api/students/{studentId}/librarycards` - we can leverage the contract itself to post against `api/librarycards` with a model that contains the student id within. This flat-route idea can simplify the implementation and aligns perfectly with the overall theme of The Standard. Keeping things simple.

3.1.1.2.1 Codes & Responses

Responses from an API controller must be mapped towards codes and responses. For instance, if we are trying to add a new student to a schooling system. We are going to `POST` student and in retrun we receive the same body we submitted with a status code `201` which means the resoruce has been `Created`.

There are three main categories where responses can fall into. The first is the success category. Where both the user and the server have done their part and the request has succeeded. The second category is the User Error Codes, where the user request has an issue of any type. In which case a `4xx` code will be returned with detailed error message to help users fix their requests for perform a successful operation. The third case is the System Error Codes, where the system has run into an issue of any type internal or external and it needs to communicate a `5xx` code to indicate to the user that something internally have gone wrong with the system and they need to contact support.

Let's talk about those codes and their scenarios in details here.

3.1.1.2.1.0 Success Codes (2xx)

Success codes either indicates a resource has been created, updated, deleted or retreived. And some cases it indicates that a request has been submitted successfully in an eventual-consistency manner that may or may not succeed in the future. Here's the details for each:

Code	Method	Details
200	Ok	Used for successful GET, PUT and DELETE operations.
201	Created	Used for successful POST operations
202	Accepted	Used for request that was delegated but may or may not succeed

Here's some examples for each:

In a retrieve non-post scenario, it's more befitting to return an Ok status code as follows:

```
[HttpGet("{studentId}")]
public async ValueTask<ActionResult<Student>> GetStudentByIdAsync(Guid studentId)
{
    Student retrievedStudent =
        await this.studentService.RetrieveStudentByIdAsync(studentId);

    return Ok(retrievedStudent);
}
```

But in a scenario where we have to create a resource, a Created is more befitting for this case as follows:

```
[HttpPost)]
public async ValueTask<ActionResult<Student>> PostStudentAsync(Student student)
{
    Student retrievedStudent =
        await this.studentService.AddStudentAsync(student);

    return Created(student);
}
```

In eventual consistency cases, where a resource posted isn't really persisted yet, we enqueue the request and return an Accepted status to indicate a process will start:

```
[HttpPost)]
public async ValueTask<ActionResult<Student>> PostStudentAsync(Student student)
{
    Student retrievedStudent =
        await this.studentEventService.EnqueueStudentEventAsync(student);

    return Accepted(student);
}
```

The Standard rule for eventual consistency scenarios is to ensure the submitter has a token of some type so requestors can inquire about the status of their request with a different API call. We will discuss these patterns in a different book called The Standard Architecture.

3.1.1.2.1.1 User Error Codes (4xx)

This is the second category of API responses. Where a user request has an issue in it and the system is required to help the user understand why their request was not successful. For instance, assume a client is submitting a new student to a schooling system. If the student Id is invalid a `400` or `Bad Request` code should be returned with a problem detail that explains what exactly is the reason for the failure of the request.

Controllers are responsible for mapping the core layer categorical exceptions into proper status codes. Here's an example:

```
[HttpGet("{studentId}")]
public async ValueTask<ActionResult<Student>> GetStudentByIdAsync(Guid studentId)
{
    try
    {
        ...
    }
    catch (StudentValidationException studentValidationException)
    {
        return BadRequest(studentValidationException.InnerException)
    }
}
```

So as shown in this code snippet, we caught a categorical validation exception and mapped it into a `400` error code which is `BadRequest`. The access to inner exception here is for the purpose of extracting a problem detail out of the `Data` property on the inner exception which contains all the dictionary values of the error report.

But sometimes controllers have to dig deeper. Catching a particular local exception not just the categorical. For instance, say we want to handle `NotFoundStudentException` with an error code `404` or `NotFound`. Here's how we would accomplish that:

```
[HttpGet("{studentId}")]
public async ValueTask<ActionResult<Student>> GetStudentByIdAsync(Guid studentId)
{
    try
    {
        ...
    }
    catch (StudentValidationException studentValidationException)
        (when studentValidationException.InnerException is NotFoundStudentException)
    {
        return NotFound(studentValidationException.InnerException)
    }
}
```

In the code snippet above, we had to examine the inner exception type to validate the localized exception from within. This is the advantage of the unwrapping and wrapping process we discussed in section 2.3.3.0.2 of The Standard. Controller may examine multiple types within the same block as well as follows:

```
...
catch (StudentCoordinationDependencyValidationException studentCoordinationDependencyValidationException)
    (when studentValidationException.InnerException
        is NotFoundStudentException
        or NotFoundLibraryCardException
        or NotFoundStudentContactException)
{
    return NotFound(studentValidationException.InnerException)
}
...
```

With that in mind, let's detail the most common mappings from exceptions to codes:

Code	Method	Exception
400	BadRequest	ValidationException or DependencyValidationException
404	NotFound	NotFoundException
409	Conflict	AlreadyExistException
423	Locked	LockedException
424	FailedDependency	InvalidReferenceException

There are more 4xx status codes out there. But As of this very moment they can either be automatically generated by the web framework like in ASP.NET or there are no useful scenarios for them yet. For instance, a 401 or Unauth orized error can be automatically generated if the controller endpoint is decorated with authorization requirement.

3.1.1.2.1.2 System Error Codes (5xx)

System error codes are the third and last possible type of codes that may occur or be returned from an API endpoint. Their main responsibility is to indicate in general that the consumer of the API endpoint is at no fault. Something bad happened in the system, and the engineering team is required to get involved to resolve the issue. That's why we log our exceptions with a severity level at the core business logic layer so we know how urgent the matter may be.

The most common http code that can be communicated on a server-side issue is the 500 or InternalServerError code. Let's take a look at a code snippet that deals with this situation:

```
[HttpGet("{studentId}")]
public async ValueTask<ActionResult<Student>> GetStudentByIdAsync(Guid studentId)
{
    try
    {
        ...
    }
    ...
    catch (StudentDependencyException studentDependencyException)
    {
        return InternalServerError(studentValidationException)
    }
}
```

In the above snippet we completely ignored the inner exception and mainly focused on the categorical exception for security reasons. Mainly to not allow internal server information to be exposed in an API response other than something as simple as `Dependency error occurred, contact support.` Since the consumer of the API is required to perform no action whatsoever other than creating a ticket for the support team.

Ideally, these issues should be caught out of Acceptance Tests which we will discuss shortly in this chapter. But there are times where there's a server blip that may cause a memory leakage of some sort or any other internal infrastrucrual issues that won't be caught by end-to-end testing in any way.

In terms of types of exceptions that may be handled, it's a little smaller when it comes server error here's the details:

Code	Method	Exception
500	InternalServerError	DependencyException or ServiceException
507	NotFound	InsufficientStorageException (Internal Only)

There's also an interesting case where two teams agree on a certain swagger document, and the back-end API development team decides to build corresponding API endpoints with methods that are not yet implemented to communicate to the other team that the work hasn't started yet. In which case using error code `501` is sufficient which is just a code for `NotImplemented`.

It is also important to mention that the native `500` error code can be communicated in ASP.NET applications through `Problem` method. We are relying on a library `RESTFulSense` to provide more codes than the native implementation can offer, but more importantly provide a problem detail serialization option and deserialization option on the client side.

3.1.1.2.1.3 All Codes

Other than the ones mentioned in previous sections, and for documentation purposes, here's the all of the 4xx and 5xx codes an API could communicate according to the latest standardized API guidelines:

Status	Code
BadRequest	400
Unauthorized	401
PaymentRequired	402
Forbidden	403
NotFound	404
NotFound	404
MethodNotAllowed	405
NotAcceptable	406
ProxyAuthenticationRequired	407
RequestTimeout	408
Conflict	409
Gone	410
LengthRequired	411
PreconditionFailed	412
RequestEntityTooLarge	413
RequestUriTooLong	414
UnsupportedMediaType	415
RequestedRangeNotSatisfiable	416
ExpectationFailed	417
MisdirectedRequest	421
UnprocessableEntity	422
Locked	423
FailedDependency	424
UpgradeRequired	426
PreconditionRequired	428
TooManyRequests	429
RequestHeaderFieldsTooLarge	431
UnavailableForLegalReasons	451
InternalServerError	500
NotImplemented	501
BadGateway	502
ServiceUnavailable	503
GatewayTimeout	504
HttpVersionNotSupported	505
VariantAlsoNegotiates	506
InsufficientStorage	507
LoopDetected	508
NotExtended	510
NetworkAuthenticationRequired	511

We will explore incorporating some of these codes in future revisions of The Standard as needed.

3.1.1.2.2 Single Dependency

Exposer components can have one and only one dependency. This dependency must be a Service component. it cannot be a Broker or any other native dependency that Brokers may use to pull configurations or any other type of dependencies.

When implementing a controller, the constructor can be implemented as follows:

```
[ApiController]
[Route("api/[controller]")]
public class StudentsController : RESTFulController
{
    private readonly IStudentService studentService;

    public StudentsController(IStudentService studentService) =>
        this.studentService = studentService;

    ...
    ...
}
```

3.1.1.2.3 Single Contract

This charactristic comes out of the box with the single dependency rule. If Services can only serve and receive one contract then the same rule will apply to controllers. They can return a contract, a list of objects with the same contract or portion of the contract when passing in Ids or queries.

3.1.1.3 Organization

Controllers should be located under `Controllers` folder and belong within a `Controllers` namespace. Controller do not need to have their own folders or namespaces as they perform a simple exposure task and that's all.

Here's an example of a controller namespace:

```
namespace GitFyle.Core.Api.Controllers
{
    [ApiController]
    [Route("api/[controller]")]
    public class ContributionsController : RESTFulController
    {
        ...
    }
}
```

3.1.1.4 Home Controller

Every system should implement an API endpoint that we call `HomeControll er`. The controller only responsibility is to return a simple message to indicate that the API is still alive. Here's an example:

```
using Microsoft.AspNetCore.Mvc;

namespace OtripleS.Web.Api.Controllers
{
    [ApiController]
    [Route("api/[controller]")]
    public class HomeController : ControllerBase
    {
        [HttpGet]
        public ActionResult<string> Get() =>
            Ok("Hello Mario, the princess is in another castle!");
    }
}
```

Home controllers are not required to have any security on them. They open a gate for heartbeat tests to ensure the system as an entity is running without checking any external dependencies. This practice is very important to help engineers know when the system is down and quickly act on it.

3.1.1.5 Tests

Controllers can be potentially unit tested to verify the mapping of exceptions to error codes are in place. But that's not a pattern I have been following myself so far. However, what is more important is Acceptance tests. Which verify all the components of the system are fully and successfully integrated with one another.

Here's an example of an acceptance test:

```
[Fact]
public async Task ShouldPostStudentAsync()
{
    // given
    Student randomStudent = CreateRandomStudent();
    Student inputStudent = randomStudent;
    Student expectedStudent = inputStudent;

    // when
    await this.otripleSApiBroker.PostStudentAsync(inputStudent);

    Student actualStudent =
        await this.otripleSApiBroker.GetStudentByIdAsync(inputStudent.Id);

    // then
    actualStudent.Should().BeEquivalentTo(expectedStudent);
    await this.otripleSApiBroker.DeleteStudentByIdAsync(actualStudent.Id);
}
```

Acceptance tests are required to cover every available endpoint on a controller. They are also responsible for cleaning up any test data after the test is completed. It is also important to mention that resources that are not owned by the microservice like database, must be emulated with applications such as WireMock and many others.

Acceptance tests are also implemented after the fact unlike unit tests. An endpoint has to be fully integrated and functional before a test is written to ensure the success of implementation is in place.

[*] Acceptance Tests (Part 1)

[*] <u>Acceptance Tests (Part 2)</u>

3.2 User Interfaces
3.2.0 Introduction

User Interfaces or UI are a type of exposer components that mainly targets humans for interaction with core business layer. Unlike Communication protocols which are mainly for distributed systems. UIs are forever evolving in terms of technologies and methedologies of which humans can interact with any given system. This goes from web applications to virtual/augmented realities. Voice activated systems and more recently brain-waves activated systems.

Developing user interfaces can be much more challenging in terms of experiences. There isn't a global standard today for what an inuitive experience is. It heavily relies on culture, commonalities and so many other forever changing variables in the world today. This Standard will outline the principles and rules for building modular, maintainable and pluggable UI components. But there will be a different Standard for outlining user experiences, human interactions and the theory of inuitiveness.

This Standard also breifly highlights certain guidelines in terms of rendering choices, server, client or hybrid as is the case with the tri-nature of everything. Let's dive deeper into the principles and rules that govern building UI components.

3.2.0.0 Principles & Rules

Just like every other exposer component type. UIs are required to be able to map processes, results and errors to their consumers. Some of these UI components will require a test-driven approach. Some others are more like Brokers where they are just wrappers around 3rd party or native UI components. Let's talk about these principles here.

3.2.0.0.0 Progress (Loading)

The most important principle in building UI component is to develop intelligence to keep the user engaged while a certain process is going. You may have seen some of these with a simple spinner or a progress bar to keep users informed at all times of what's going on behind the scenes in the system.

It's a violation of The Standard to indicate a progress of any type if nothing really is going in the background. It falls into the practice of wasting end-users time and basically lying to them about the actual status of the system. But assuming the system is actually busy working on a certain request, there are three levels of communication that can happen on an exposer component to communicate a progress. Let's discuss those in detail:

3.2.0.0.0.0 Basic Progress

The basic progress approach is where you present a status with a label like "Waiting ..." or a spinner with no further indication. This is the bare minimum of progress indication and no UI should just freeze or stop their hanging while requests are being processed in the background assuming an eventual-consistency pattern is not attainable for the current business need.

Some web applications choose to show a forever progress bar at the very top of the page to indicate a progress is happening. From an experience perspective and depending on the visibilty level of these progress bars it may or may not be easy to miss by end users. Some other engineering teams have chosen to play a simple animation to keep users engaged with visual progress without any indication of the details of that progress.

3.2.0.0.0.1 Remaining Progress

A bit above the bare minimum, there are indication of remaining time or remaining progress to be completed before the request is processed. An indication such as "40% remaining" or something more specific like "5 minutes remaining ..." to help end-users understand or guestimate how long time or effort is left. There are patterns where engineers would indicate how tasks are left without any indication of what these tasks are.

Sometimes a reamining progress update is as detailed as UI engineers can get. For instance, if you are downloading a file from the internet. You can't be more detailed than saying x percent of the bits remaining to be downloaded with no further details. Some game developers choose to also visualize the internet speeds and available disk space all to just keep the end-user engaged in the system. And these are all acceptable pattern in this Standard.

3.2.0.0.0.2 Detailed Progress

The highest level of reporting progress is the detailed progress type. Where the UI component is fully transparent with it's consumers by reporting every step of progress. This type of progress is more common in scientific applications. Engineers in debugging mode may enable a feature where all the underlying activity in the system is visualized through the UI.

This type helps end-users understand what is happening behind the scenes but also allows them to communicate better details to support engineers to help them fix an issue if the process happens to fail. But this process isn't always preferred in terms of experience considering that some details needs to be hidden for security reasons.

In summary, selecting the right type of progress in UI is mainly dependant on the business flow, type of users who will interact with the system and several other variable which we will be discussing in The Experience Standard.

3.2.0.0.1 Results

UI exposer components will report a result to indicate the completion of a certain request by end-users. Consider registering a new student in a schooling system. There are several ways to indicate the registration process have been completed successfully. Let's discuss those type of results visualization in detail here.

3.2.0.0.1.0 Simple

The simple indication of success is when the UI reports that the process was completed successfully without any further details. You may have seen some of these implementations for this type such as "Thank you, request submitted" or something as simple as a checkmark with a visualization of green color that indicates success in some way.

Simple results indications especially with submitted requests than retrieved data may add some more details in terms of the next course of action.

3.2.0.0.1.1 Partial Details

The other type of results or success indication is present end-users with partial details. An overview of the nature of the request, where it stands in terms of status and timestamps. Partial details are usually useful when it comes to providing the end-user with a "ticket number" to help end-users follow up on their requests later to inquire about the status. This pattern is very common in e-commerce applications where every purchase request may be returned with a tracking number to help customers and customer support personnel assess with the requests.

Partial detailed results can also be very helpful for the visualiztion of the success process. Especially with requests that contains multiple parts. Larger requests such as submitting an application to join a university or the likes, it may contain attachments, multiple pages of details and confidential information such as payment details or social security numbers.

3.2.0.0.1.2 Full Details

In some cases, it might also be preferred to report full details about the submitted request. Especially with smaller requests where it may be useful to help end-users review their requests. Some engineers prefer to display full details as an extra confirmational step before actually submitting the request. But full details can also include more than just the request details, it could include status update from the server a long with assigned point of contact or an officer from maintenance and support teams.

It's a violation of The Standard to redirect end-users at the submittal of their requests with no indication of what happened.

3.2.0.0.2 Error Reports

Error reports main responsibility is to inform end-users of what happened, why it happened and what's the next course of action. Some types of error reports don't necessarily indicate any course of action which can be a poor exprience depending on the business flow. But the bare minimum in error reporting is the basic indication of the error itself with basic details. Let's talk about those types in here.

3.2.0.0.2.0 Informational

The bare minimum of error reports is the informational type. Indicating an error occurred and why it occurred. Something like: "Request failed. Try again" or "Request failed, contract support". There are also informational errors that are time based. Something like: "Our servers are currently experiencing a high volume of requests. Please try again later". These informational error reports are necessary to keep the end-user engaged in consuming the system in anyway.

Informational error reports are governed by the context and the type of users receiving them. In a scientific application the more details the better. For some other systems, it is important to shift the technical language of the errors to a more less technical language. For instance, we can't communicate: "Student Id cannot be null, empty or widespace". We should select a more readable language such as: "Please provide a valid student Id".

3.2.0.0.2.1 Referencial/Implicit Actions

The second type of error reports are the referencial type. When an erro occurs, it automatically take the action of informing the support team and returns a reference of a support ticket to end users so they can follow up on. You may see this a lot when video games fail to start, or certain applications is unable to initialize. Referencial error reports are the best when it comes certain business flows, since it takes care of all the actions, sends an email to the end user with the reference number then just follows up within a couple of days to report the status.

In general the less actions a certain system may require it's users to take after a certain failure has occurred, the better. Since end-users have already accomplished their tasks in terms of submitting requests. It becomes even more convenient if the original request is queued up such as the case with high volume enterprise systems so end-users don't have to re-submit the same data.

3.2.0.0.2.2 Actionable

The second type of error reports is the actionable reports. Errors that occur and provide an additional action for the users to go further in their request. For instance, there are error reports that will provide a button to try again. Or submitting an additional details request back to the engineering and support teams.

There are also reports that will provide a different route to accomplish the same task in more hybrid legacy and modernized applications. These actionable reports are more convenient than the informational reports, but they would still require their end-users to take more actions, more key strokes which leads to a certain level of inconvenience.

3.2.0.0.3 Single Dependency

As is the case with any exposer component. it can only be integrated with a single dependency at all times. However, in the case of UI components, there is always the contract purity case where the UI is not supposed to be given more than what it needs in terms of data. This is where a new type of foundational-like services are implemented to ensure this pattern is enforced and all other details such as audit fields, timestamps and such are taken care of away from the UI component sight.

We will talk in detail about view services shortly as we progress talking about UI exposers.

3.2.0.0.4 Anatomy

Just like the data flow in any service. We have brokers -> Services -> Exposers. UI components also form their own data flow in terms of rendering. let's take a look at the anatomy of UI exposers in this illustration:

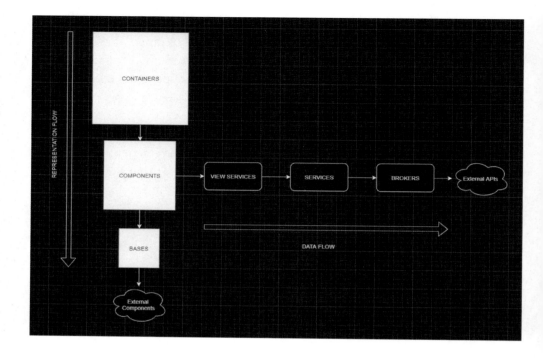

UI exposer components as shown above can be Bases, Components or Containers. Each one of these types has a specific responsibility to ensure the maintainbility and pluggability of the system is at it's highest scores according to The Standard. Let's discuss these three types here:

3.2.0.0.4.0 Bases

Base or Base Components are just like Brokers in the data flow. They are simple thin wrappers around native or 3rd party components. Their main responsibility is to abstract away the hard dependency on non-local components to allow the configurability of the system to switch to any other external or native UI components with the least effort possible.

Base components also makes it easier to mock out any external or native components behavior, and focuses the effort on ensuring the local component is performing the way its expected. We will discuss in the next chapter base components for web applications in Blazor and other technologies.

3.2.0.0.4.1 Components

UI Components are a hybrid between a Service and a Controller in the data pipeline. In a way components contain *some* business logic in terms of handling interactions with certain base components. But they are also limited by integrating with one and only one view service. Components are test-driven, they require writing tests to ensure they behave as expected. But they also contain almost no iteration, selection or sequencing data logic within them.

The most important aspect about UI components is that they are at the intersection between the UI flow and the data flow. They are responsible for leveraging their data dependency (view services) and their base components to become easily pluggable into container components (like pages with routes in web applications).

3.2.0.0.4.2 Containers

Container components are orchestrators/aggregators of components. They are the actual route or the page end-users interact with. Containers cannot have any level of UI logic in them. They cannot leverage base components. And they may have any number of UI components as the business flow requires.

As it is the case with every category of components, containers cannot integrate with other containers. The rule applies across the board for every data or UI component of any type.

3.2.0.0.5 UI Component Types

UI components come in all different shapes and sizes. The hosting environment and the type of devices that serve these components play a big role in determining the technologies and the capabilities a certain UI component may have. Let's talk about the different types of UI components in this section.

3.2.0.0.5.0 Web Applications

The most popular type of UI applications are web apps. Web applications are the most popular and dominant due to their ease-of-use. They require no installation of any kind. They have no dependency on the operating system running the system or the type of devices users may be using. They can run on PCs, tablets, mobile phones and even TVs and watches that support web browsing.

In the last few years, web frameworks have evolved a lot due to the aforementioned popularity. There are frameworks that allow engineers to write web applications in so many programming languages today. The web assembly evolution have also opened the door for engineers to develop even more scalable frameworks with their preferred technologies and languages.

Web applications are developed in two different types in terms of rendering. Server-side applications and client-side applications. We will discuss the advantages and disadvantages of each type in addition to the hybrid model in the next few chapters of The Standard.

3.2.0.0.5.1 Mobile Applications

The second most popular platform today to develop UIs is the mobile world. Developing mobile applications comes with its own set of challenges as they are heavily dependant on the operating system, the size of the phone in terms of resolution and the available native controls. Mobile applications are also always client-side apps. They are just like Desktop applications, they require to be compiled, provisioned and published to an app store so consumers can download them, install them and leverage them in their daily activities.

The biggest advantage of mobile applications is that they allow for offline interactions. Like mobile games, editing apps and streaming services with offline capabilities. But building mobile applications with web frameworks is becoming more and more popular. The universal eco-system that allows end-users to experience software the same way on their PCs, browsers and mobile applications the exact same way. This trend shall eventually allow engineers to develop systems for all different eco-systems at least cost possible.

3.2.0.0.5.2 Other Types

There are other types for UI components that we may not cover in our Standard. These types are like, console/terminal applications, desktop applications, video games and virtual/augmented reality software in addition to wearable devices and voice activated systems. The world of Human-Machine-Interface HMI is evolving so rapidly in the age of metaverse that we might need to create at some point special chapters for these different types.

3.2.1 Web Applications
3.2.1.0 Introduction

Web applications are the most common type of exposer components today. They are much more easier to use than any other known exposer UI component in the software industry. But more importantly, web applications have much more divrse set of technologies than mobile applications. The web software market is also much easier for engineer to publish to and update than mobile applications which makes it quite attractive for newer engineers in general.

In this chapter, we will be using Blazor technology to demonstrate implementing The Standard principles for web applications. But as I previously mentioned, The Standard is technology-agnostic. Which means it can be applied to any web technology without any issues.

3.2.1.1 On the Map

Web applications usually set at the other end of any system. They are the terminals that humans use to interact with the system. Let's take a look at where they are located on the map:

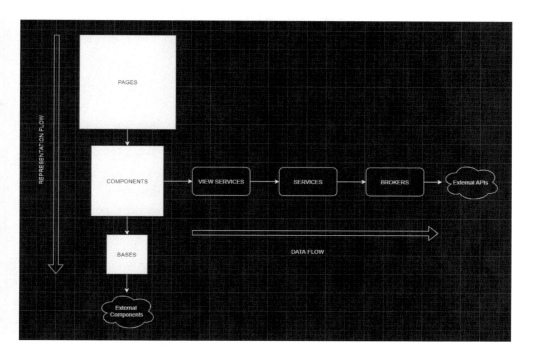

As shown above, web applications are somewhat similar to core APIs, except that they have a different group of components in terms of visualization such as Pages, Components and Bases. There's an intersection between two main flows in every web application. The presentation flow and the data/business flow. Depending on where a web application lives in terms of high-level architecture it's location determines whether it's backend (BFF or Backend of Frontend) is a business flow or just data flow. Let's discuss these details in the characteristics section in this chapter.

3.2.1.2 Charactristics

Web applications are usually 6 basic components. Brokers, Services, View Services, Bases, Components and Pages. Since we've already discussed the data flow components in the Services portion of The Standard. In this section, we will be discussing the UI aspect (Bases, Components and Pages) with a slight detail about view services.

Let's discuss these charactristic here.

3.2.1.2.0 Anatomy

UI components consist of base, components and pages. They all play the role of separating the responsibility of integration, rendering and routing users to a particular UI functionality.

Let's talk about these types in detail.

3.2.1.2.0.0 Base Component

Base components are just like brokers, they are wrappers around native or external UI components. Their main responsbility is to abstract away any hard dependency on non-local UI capability. For instance, let's say we want to offer the capability to create text boxes for data insertion/capture. The native <input> tag could offer this capability. But exposing or leveraging this tag in our core UI components is dangerous. Because it creates a hard dependency on non-abstract UI components. If we decide at any point in time to use some 3rd party UI component, we would need to change these native <input> tags across all the components that use them. That's not an optimum strategy.

Let's take a look at a visualization for base component functionality:

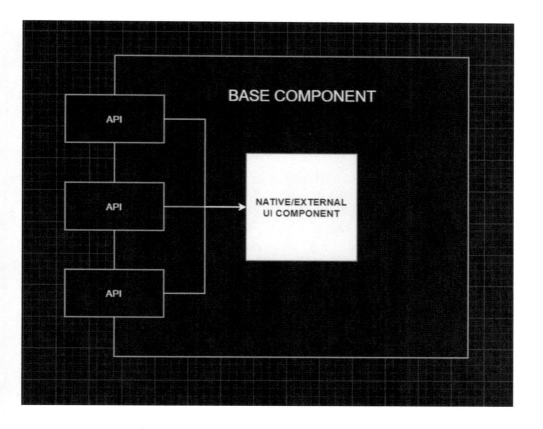

As seen the above example, base components will wrap an external or native UI component then expose APIs to allow the interaction with that component seamlessly and programmatically. There are occasions where these APIs will represent parameters, functions or delegates to interact with the component based on the business flow.

3.2.1.2.0.0.0 Implementation

Let's take a look at a simple Base component for solving this problem:

```
<input @bind-value=Value />

public partial class TextBoxBase : ComponentBase
{
    [Parameter]
    public string Value {get; set;}

    public void SetValue(string value) =>
        this.Value = value;
}
```

In the code above, we wrapped the `<input>` tag with our own base component `TextBoxBase` and we offered an input parameter `Value` to be passed into that component so it can pass it down to the native UI element. Additionally, we also provided a public function `SetValue` to allow for programmatically mimicking the users behavior to test drive the consuming component of this base element.

3.2.1.2.0.0.1 Utilization

Now, when we try to leverage this base component at the core components level we can simply call it as follows:

```
<TextBoxBase @ref=MyTextBox />
```

The `@ref` aspect will allow the backend code to interact with the base component programmatically behind the scenes to call any existing functionality.

3.2.1.2.0.0.2 Restrictions

Base components can only be used by Core components or just components for short. They may not be used by pages and they may not be used by other Base components. But more importantly, it's preferred that base components would only wrap around one and only one non-local component.

And just like Brokers, Base Components do not have any logic in them. They don't handle exceptions, do any calculations or any form of sequential, iterative or selective business logic operations. These operations are either data-based where they belong to view services and downstream APIs or UI-based where they belong to Core Components.

Base components also don't handle exceptions, they don't throw their own exceptions and they don't perform any type of validations.

3.2.1.2.0.1 Core Component

Core components are just like services in the data flow. They are test-driven but they are also restricted with one and only one dependency at all times. Core components leverage Base components to perform a business-specific flow. They are less generic than Base components because they orchestrate and communicate with the data flow.

Here's a visualization of core components architecture:

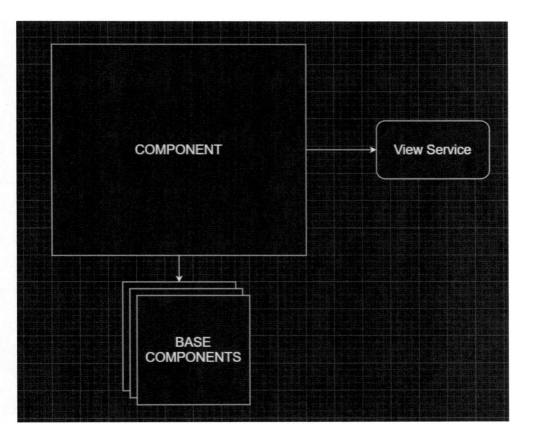

Core components in a way are orchestrators of UI and Data components. They will leverage one or many Base components to construct a business specific flow such as a student registration form then send the signal to view services to persist that data and return responses or report errors.

3.2.1.2.0.1.0 Implementation & Tests

Let's take a look at the implementation of a core component.

```
public partial class StudentRegistrationComponent : ComponentBase
{
    [Inject]
    public IStudentViewService StudentViewService {get; set;}

    public StudentRegistrationComponentState State {get; set;}
    public StudentView StudentView {get; set;}
    public TextBoxBase StudentNameTextBox {get; set;}
    public ButtonBase SubmitButton {get; set;}
    public LabelBase StatusLabel {get; set;}

    public void OnIntialized() =>
        this.State == StudentRegisterationComponentState.Content;

    public async Task SubmitStudentAsync()
    {
        try
        {
            this.StudentViewService.AddStudentViewAsync(this.StudentView);
        }
        catch (Exception exception)
        {
            this.State = StudentRegisterationComponentState.Error;
        }
    }
}
```

The above code shows thee different types of properties within any given component, The dependency view service which maps raw API models/data into consumable UI models. And the `State` which determines whether a component should be `Loading`, `Content` or `Error`. The data view model to bind incoming input to one unified model `StudentView`. And the last three are Base level components which are used to construct the form of registration.

Let's take a look at the markup side of the core component:

```
<Condition Evaluation=IsLoading>
    <Match>
        <LabelBase @ref=StatusLabel Value="Loading ..." />
    </Match>
</Condition>

<Condition Evaluation=IsContent>
    <Match>
        <TextBoxBase @ref=StudentNameTextBox @bind-value=StudentView.Name />
        <ButtonBase @ref=SubmitButton Label="Submit" OnClick=SubmitStudentAsync />
    </Match>
</Condition>

<Condition Evaluation=IsError>
    <Match>
        <LabelBase @ref=StatusLabel Value="Error Occurred" />
    </Match>
</Condition>
```

We linked the references of the student registeration component properties to UI components to ensure the rendering of these components have actually occurred and the submission of data has been executed.

Let's take a look at a couple of tests to verify these states. a component has already loaded state. And post submission states.

```
[Fact]
public void ShouldRenderComponent()
{
    // given
    StudentRegisterationComponentState expectedComponentState =
        StudentRegisterationComponentState.Content;

    // when
    this.renderedStudentRegistrationComponent =
        RenderComponent<StudentRegistrationComponent>();

    // then
    this.renderedStudentRegistrationComponent.Instance.StudentView
        .Should().NotBeNull();

    this.renderedStudentRegistrationComponent.Instance.State
        .Should().Be(expectedComponentState);

    this.renderedStudentRegistrationComponent.Instance.StudentNameTextBox
        .Should().NotBeNull();

    this.renderedStudentRegisterationComponent.Instance.SubmitButton
        .Should().NotBeNull();

    this.renderedStudentRegistrationComponent.Instance.StatusLabel.Value
        .Should().BeNull();

    this.studentViewServiceMock.VerifyNoOtherCalls();
}
```

The test above will verify that all the components are assigned a reference property and no external dependency calls have been made. it validates that the code in the `OnIntialized` function on the component level is validated and performing as expected.

Now, let's take a look at the submittal code validations:

```
[Fact]
public void ShouldSubmitStudentAsync()
{
    // given
    StudentRegisterationComponentState expectedComponentState =
        StudentRegisterationComponentState.Content;

    var inputStudentView = new StudentView
    {
        Name = "Hassan Habib"
    };

    StudentView expectedStudentView = inputStudentView;

    // when
    this.renderedStudentRegistrationComponent =
        RenderComponent<StudentRegistrationComponent>();

    this.renderedStudentRegistrationComponent.Instance.StudentName
        .SetValue(inputStudentView.Name);

    this.renderedStudentRegistrationComponent.Instance.SubmitButton.Click();

    // then
    this.renderedStudentRegistrationComponent.Instance.StudentView
        .Should().NotBeNull();

    this.renderedStudentRegisterationComponent.Instance.StudentView
        .Should().BeEquivalentTo(expectedStudentView);

    this.renderedStudentRegistrationComponent.Instance.State
        .Should().Be(expectedComponentState);

    this.renderedStudentRegistrationComponent.Instance.StudentNameTextBox
        .Should().NotBeNull();

    this.renderedStudentRegistrationComponent.Instance.StudentNameTextBox.Value
        .Should().BeEquivalentTo(studentView.Name);

    this.renderedStudentRegisterationComponent.Instance.SubmitButton
        .Should().NotBeNull();

    this.renderedStudentRegistrationComponent.Instance.StatusLabel.Value
        .Should().BeNull();

    this.studentViewServiceMock.Verify(service =>
        service.AddStudentAsync(inputStudentView),
            Times.Once);

    this.studentViewServiceMock.VerifyNoOtherCalls();
}
```

The test above validates that on submittal, the student model is populated
with the data set programmatically through base component instance, but
also verifies all these components are actually rendered on the screen before
end-users by validating each base component has an assigned instance on
runtime or render-time.

3.2.1.2.0.1.1 Restrictions

Core components have similar restrictions to Base components in a way they
cannot call each other at that level. There's a level of Orchestration Core
Components that can combine multiple components to exchange messages
but they don't render anything on their own the same way Orchestration
services delegate all the work to their dependencies.

But Core components also are not allowed to call more then one and only one
view service. And in that, they stay true to the view model at all times. One
views service corresponds to one core component which renders one and
only one view model.

View services may do their own orchestration-level work as well, in an extremely complex flow but it's highly recommend to keep things at a flat level. These very same view services perform nothing but mapping and adding audit fields in addition to basic structural validations.

3.2.1.2.0.2 Pages

In every web application, pages are a very fundamental mandatory container component that needs to exist so end-users could navigate to them. Pages mainly hold a route, communicate a paramter from that route and combine core-level components to represents a business value.

A good example for pages are dashboards. Dashboard pages are a container of multiple components like tiles, notifications, headers and side bars with references to other pages. Pages don't hold any business logic in and of themselves, but they delegate all route-related operations to their child components.

Let's take a look at a simple page implementation:

```
@page '/registration'

<HeaderComponent />
<StudentRegisterationComponent />
<FooterComponent />
```

Pages are much simpler than core or base components. They don't require unit testing, and they don't necessarily need a backend code. They just purely reference their components without reference (unless needed) and they help serve that content when a route is navigated to.

3.2.1.2.0.3 Unobtrusiveness

For all UI components, it's a violation to include code from multiple technologies/languages in the same page. For instance, a CSS style code, C# code and HTML markup cannot all exist at the same file. They need to separated in their own files.

The unobtrusiveness rule helps prevent cognitive pollution for engineers building UI components, but also makes the system much easier to maintain. That's why every component can nest it's files beneath it if the IDE/ Environment used for development allows for partial implementations as follows:

- StudentRegisterationComponent.razor
    - StudentRegisterationComponent.razor.cs
    - StudentRegisterationComponent.razor.css

The node file here `.razor` file has all the markup needed to kick off the initialization of the component. While both nested files are supporting files for simple UI logic code and styling. With this level of organization (especially in Blazor) doesn't require any referencing for these nested/support files. This may not be the case for other technologies so I urge engineers to do their very best to fit that model/Standard.

3.2.1.2.0.4 Organization

All UI components are listed under a Views folder in the solution. let's take a look:

- Views
  - Bases
  - Components
  - Pages

This tri-nature conforming organization should make it easier to shift reusable components and make it also easier to find these components based on their categories. I will leave it up to the preference of the engieneers to determine whether to break down these components further by folders/ namespaces or leave them all at the same level given the nesting is in place.

Made in the USA
Middletown, DE
16 October 2022

12481603R00095